C. Bishop '82

THE JOURNALS OF
SAMUEL RUTHERFORD DUNDASS

&

GEORGE KELLER
CROSSING THE PLAINS
TO CALIFORNIA IN 1849-1850

THE JOURNAL OF SAMUEL RUTHERFORD DUNDASS

CROSSING THE PLAINS TO CALIFORNIA IN

1849

YE GALLEON PRESS
FAIRFIELD, WASHINGTON

Library of Congress Cataloging in Publication Data

Main entry under title:

The Journals of Samuel Rutherford Dundass & George Keller.

The journal of George Keller originally published as: A trip across the plains and life in California.
    Includes index.
    Contents: The journal of Samuel Rutherford Dundass — The journal of George Keller.
    1. West (U.S.) — Description and travel — 1848-1860. 2. California — Description and travel — 1848-1869. 3. Overland journeys to the Pacific. 4. Dundass, Samuel Rutherford, 1819-1850. 5. Keller, George. I. Dundass, Samuel Rutherford, 1819-1850. Journal of Samuel Rutherford Dundass. 1983. II. Keller, George. Trip across the plains and life in California. 1983.
F593.J68   1983   917.8'042   83-3678
ISBN 0-87770-291-8

TABLE OF CONTENTS

JOURNAL

OF

SAMUEL RUTHERFORD DUNDASS,

FORMERLY

AUDITOR OF JEFFERSON COUNTY, OHIO,

INCLUDING HIS

ENTIRE ROUTE TO CALIFORNIA,

AS A MEMBER OF THE

Steubenville Company bound for San Francisco,

IN THE YEAR 1849.

————————

STEUBENVILLE, O.
PRINTED AT CONN'S JOB OFFICE.
1857.

INTRODUCTION

On the 24th of March, 1849, there was more than ordinary excitement in the usually quiet, and beautiful city of Steubenville. A company had been organized during the previous winter, for the golden regions on the shores of the Pacific Ocean. Wonderful news from California had reached the enterprising inhabitants of the Buckeye State. Texas had been annexed to this mighty confederacy, the Mexican war had passed away, and with its transit, California too, came knocking for admission into this "glorious union." Inexhaustible treasures are soon discovered in its mountains and vallies, and in the very beds of those rivers whose history is lost in the dark recesses of the primeval generations of men. What an intense excitement pervades the American continent! What multitudes are attracted to these far distant regions, corresponding in their atmosphere and scenery, to oriental climes! What complicated motives animate the thousands young and old, who enter the line of march for this modern land of promise; some to procure an earthly independence, some as a desperate remedy for impaired health, and others no doubt, to carry with them, the elements of Christianity and literature and civilization into that region of the earth, so abundant in facilities, to exert the mightiest influence for good on the millions of the old world. Hence with all that seemed visionary in the enterprise, with all its gaudy castles in the air, and with all the disastrous results, foreseen by reflecting men, from lofty, and falling and fallen superstructures, which from the first, had nothing but a foundation of sand for their support; with all these barriers in the way, the immense movement towards California, had the sympathy of the best men in the land. In this phenomenon of emigration, they recognized in a moment, the hand of an infinitely wise and superintending providence. They saw God moving in a "mysterious way, his wonders to perform." And this land of gold might become the grave of thousands, and like the battle of Waterloo, clothe unnumbered multitudes in mourning; still through the victims thus sacrificed in the conflict, through the dark vista of the future, the friends of truth and humanity, saw civil and religious liberty widely extended, and the dominion of King Emanuel, built up on the Earth.

On the Sabbath evening previous to the embarkation of the Steubenville company, its members marched in a body, to one of the Churches of the city, and were addressed in the most solemn and appropriate language, by Rev. Dr. Beatty, and Rev. Mr. Nicholson, a clergyman of the Methodist Episcopal Church. And on the following Monday, as they embarked on the noble steamer ready for their

7

accommodation, they were favored with an eloquent oration by Col. George W. McCook. Numbers of citizens flocked to the wharf to bid farewell to friends, and with a hearty "God bless you," to be impressed with the conviction, that they might return no more forever.

Col. James Collier, of Steubenville, having received the appointment of Collector of the Revenue for Upper California, made his way with all possible expedition to the place of his destination. And it was well for many a young emigrant, that the Col. occupied a position so important and influential. He was known in California, as the friend of the needy and destitute in general; but the sympathies of his benevolent heart especially overflowed to those young men from his own region of country, who had suffered the "loss of all things," in passing through the wilderness, to the land of gold. His kind offices in behalf of Samuel R. Dundass, the writer of the following Journal, are still held in grateful remembrance by surviving friends, while the hand that first recorded them, is mouldering in the grave. In the city of Buffalo, on his way home to the bosom of his friends, the stern arrest of death was laid on him whose Journal is now given to the public. It was not originally designed for publication, and being written under the most unfavorable circumstances, it of course assumes nothing in the way of pretension to literary merit, and is now committed to the press, with all its imperfections, as at least some humble memorial of one who is "not lost, but gone before."

JOURNAL OF S.R. DUNDASS

CHAPTER ONE

Journey from Steubenville to Independence.

ARCH 24, 1849.—Embarked at Steubenville on board the steamboat *Germantown*, associated with 59 others from Steubenville and vicinity, organized as a "California Mining Company." The vessel was extremely crowded; still we had no steamboat disaster, and but little to mar the pleasure of our trip down the beautiful Ohio; and on the first of April, we landed at St. Louis.

APRIL 3.—Reshipped, and proceeded on the steamer *Mary Blane*, bound for Independence, Mo., and in four days we arrived at the place of our destination, landing on the banks of the Missouri River, about three miles from Independence. It was Saturday and advanced in the evening, and the landing very muddy. We went into camp immediately on the river bank, some fifty rods below the landing, and after storing our provision, and conveying our baggage to camp, through a drenching rain, repaired to our tents at a late hour, to test the luxury of a bed of Buffalo skins for which our evening's exercise had admirably prepared us.

We were up early on the morning of the 8th, preparing our Breakfast, and making our best demonstration in the art of cooking. On the 10th of April, we removed to the brow of the river hill, where we had a good camp, and remained until the 24th, completing our outfit, procuring oxen and robes, and everything necessary for a final debut on the immense plains spread out before us.

CHAPTER TWO

Journey from Independence to the Platte River.

On the morning of the 24th, we were up at an early hour and actively engaged in preparing to march. We had calculated on an early start, but found it far advanced in the day before we got off, owing chiefly to some difficulty in yoking and assigning the ox teams to the different messes. Our oxen had been bought in the neighborhood, and turned loose in a large field near our camp, where we fed them on corn, and being strange to each other, and many of us total strangers to driving, we made as might be expected, rather a novel movement. One drove against a tree, another barely escaped upsetting. The team of another manifested a strange disposition to take the other end of the road, and several men were required to prevent the animals from taking this stubborn course. I was fortunately not on the list of drivers that morning, as I would doubtless have sustained a loss of reputation in reference to the appropriate qualifications for such a *classical* service, had our team proved as refractory with me as it did with the person driving it: for, by some means our wagon tongue was broken before we got out of camp. Providentially however, we had a wagon maker in our mess; and in a few hours we had this indispensable appendage of our ox locomotive replaced, and were after the train which had now all got off in advance of us. It was in the afternoon when we left, and we had ten miles to travel before reaching the place selected for our next encampment. We reached the desirable spot awhile after dark, and found all safely in but one wagon which we passed a short distance from camp. The hounds of this vehicle had been broken in crossing a deep ravine on the borders of a prairie, and was from the necessity of the case, left under guard till the next morning, when it was repaired and brought into camp. We remained in camp, until noonday on the 25th, when we were all ready for marching, and left in regular train for Blue river—10 miles distant. We made quite an imposing appearance, with twenty large, covered, six ox wagons, and sixty men armed and equipped according to western style.

We encamped in the evening, a mile east of Blue river, on a beautiful prairie, and near a spring of excellent water. Our oxen were turned out awhile to graze, and then put into a small fenced lot for the night, and fed on corn, the staple production of the country, procured with facility at any point of the road, at twenty-five or thirty cents per bushel, which indeed is a higher rate than usual, on account of the increased demand occasioned by the large number of emigrants en route for the land of gold, and for other places towards the setting sun.

Finding the grass not sufficiently advanced for forage, we determined to remain in the vicinity and feed corn until we could proceed in safety to our oxen; accordingly we selected a convenient camp west of the river, where we had pasture, wood and water in an enclosure, and remained there until the 30th, making some alterations on our wagons, procuring corn, and attending to other requisites for the successful prosecution of our journey over the plains.

APRIL 30.—Left early in the morning and marched sixteen miles, which brought us properly on the prairies, and nothing was wanting to render the scene enchanting, but a supply of water the want of which we sensibly felt before night, as we passed none during the day but a pond of muddy water in a small ravine that afforded a scanty supply only for the oxen. The poor animals in our service, had the preference of access to the water for the simple reason that the men could not use it. We arrived before sunset at lone elm encampment, and stopped for the night. The encampment is so called from an elm that stands almost in the bed of the small stream affording water of tolerable quality. It is the only tree for miles around, and is an object of curiosity to all who pass by; it is about three feet in diameter, of medium height, and has had a beautiful spreading top, the limbs of which however, have been cut off within the last few years by emigrants for camp fires, and the venerable tree is now on the decline. We found no wood here, and our only resort was to some empty barrels in our wagons, and some dry weeds. We dug small trenches in the ground, and by building our fires in them, secured the full benefit of our small stock of fuel. The night was very cold and windy, but our day's labor had prepared us for a good night's repose even in a cotton tent, with bedding of Buffalo skins and blankets. Enclosures had been procured at our previous camps for our cattle, but we now commenced herding them on the Prairie. This was done by assigning them sufficient space on which to graze, and keeping them together by a guard.

MAY 1.—Rose early, and were on our way a little after "sun up." We left to-day, the great Santa Fe thoroughfare, one of the best natural roads in the world, extending through a vast extent of Prairie, so level that the dashing rains which wash, and keep constantly out of repair, roads in more hilly countries, have no effect on this great highway of nature, but to produce a little mud for a few hours, when the water disappears being absorbed by the peculiar soil on which it descends. This soil is of a sandy and loose texture, and very deep, covered at this season of the year with a beautiful coat of deep green, variegated with delicious flowers. Whatever emotions of the beautiful, the grand, the sublime, different persons may have on first viewing and travelling over those plains so properly denominated the "Eden of the West," one impression must press itself on every reflecting mind, *viz*: their vast agricultural resources; let them be but fully developed, and North America is second to no other country on the earth. She has

11

amply sufficient for herself and a surplus for the world. We encamped this evening on Bull Creek, having travelled sixteen miles. We found but a meagre supply of water during the day; but had both wood and water here, as the creek is skirted slightly with woodland. In pitching our tents, but few of them were trenched, which was soon found to be an essential security against rain. During the first part of the night, the clouds poured down torrents of water, accompanied by the lightning's flash and the thunder's roar, leaving a number without any resort for beds but their wagons.

We were up early on the morning of the 2d, and prepared to move on; but unfortunately broke a wagon tongue while leaving camp, which detained us until near nine o'clock. Wm. Hays, one of our company had gone back on a dispatch, from Blue River to Independence, three days before, for some articles, the company had neglected to secure, and not having yet overtaken us, two others were sent this morning to meet him. They met him a few miles back, and all overtook the train during the day. Our friend Hays had been overtaken by the storm during the night previous, and had spent it, with his horse on the open plain. We encamped in the evening at 4 o'clock, having travelled only eight miles since we started in the morning. The stream on which we encamped, afforded an abundance of water, and having some timber along its course, offers strong inducements to the emigrant to stop for the night at whatever hour in the day he may reach it. The Prairie near this stream assumes a bluff appearance, which viewed from a distance looks like small regular mountains. One to the right of the road near our camp, attracted particular attention, and a number of our company made the ascent to the summit, from which they obtained a grand view of the surrounding country. It is of a regular conical shape, rising gradually from the level of the plain, and terminating in a beautiful round vertex or top. Indications of stone coal were found about the banks of this stream, and a small vein of excellent coal had already been discovered.

MAY 3. — Were up and on march at an early hour, but a cold and incessant rain rendered it uncomfortable for the men and slippery and laborious for the oxen. We came to the Chawowow River in the forenoon, in the crossing of which we were detained several hours. The stream is something like our largest sized creeks in the States; but being considerably swollen from recent rains, was now very high and scarcely fordable at all. The banks were steep and abounding in the deepest mud, and the road extremely narrow. We were compelled to let our wagons down by a long cable, and double our teams in ascending the opposite bank. As the process of driving up proved much slower than the descent we soon formed a close train in the bottom, where we had to drive up the current for some distance before reaching the point from which the road left the river; and as the foremost teams were detained assisting the others up the bank, those immediately behind them, were obliged to stand in the water with their teams, until those before them could advance out of their way. After several hours hard labor, we all got over this river, fed our oxen, and went three miles further where we encamped on a high limestone bluff, at the base of which we obtained tolerably good water, but no fuel except dry weeds and some other apologies for wood, sufficient to prepare a cup of coffee which we relished well; and to which we did ample justice after the exposure and fatigue of the day. It continued to rain for the most part during the night, and although the road is sandy and dry, it had now become quite muddy and heavy for the wagons. We had only come ten miles yesterday and wishing to make up our deficit to-day, we were on our journey earlier than usual, and traveled without interruption all day; but after passing through the descending rain we only made twelve miles towards the place of our destination. Encamped at 5 P.M., at a place of general stopping, where we found some scattering timber, and a good supply of water from a source apparently the head of a stream which bore off in a northwesterly direction, marked in its course by a beautiful woodland.

We had met some Indians on yesterday and this evening saw a number pass our camp of the Caw tribe as far as we could ascertain.

MAY 6. — Travelled eighteen miles to Wolf Creek, where we encamped until the 8th, the seventh being the Sabbath day. Its sacred associations are even here with us in the wilderness, and God forbid that we should ever desecrate it. This Creek has a beautiful range of woodland, a few rods wide, along its course, which was now in full bloom, and together with a number of bluffs and mounds around its banks, all dressed with the surrounding plain in nature's brightest, most enchanting colors, and washed by the recent rains, all combined, spread out before us a landscape, rarely excelled in grandeur; and the scene brightens, as the setting sun shed his last rays through broken clouds that floated slowly in the west, as if lingering to gild their borders in his golden beams. The full moon had just risen in the east, and poured a flood of silvery light upon the earth and sky, giving additional radiance to the scene, presenting even in the western wilds of America a twilight that would vie with an Italian eve.

MAY 8. — Proceeded to Kansas river, where finding several trains of wagons before us, waiting to cross, we encamped for the day.

Our company had organized for the purpose of emigrating together, and mining in California as a Joint Stock So. But having become impressed with the conviction that small trains could travel much faster than large ones, and other circumstances being favorable to a dissolution, a meeting of the company was called, and a resolution adopted to dissolve into companies of tens, making an equitable division of the general stock on hands. We crossed the Kansas to-

13

gether on the 9th, and encamped three miles from the river, where we remained until the 12th, dividing our teams, wagons and provisions. Leaving our encampment on the afternoon of the 12th, we marched ten miles to a creek where we found considerable difficulty in crossing on account of a heavy rain that fell during the afternoon and made the banks of the creek, which are generally steep, very slippery and dangerous. Three of our number, Burgett, Anderson and myself had left the train for an Indian village some five miles from the main road, with a view to procure some articles of Merchandize to be found there. The village is constituted of a few Indian huts and log cabins, with two or three small stores, reasonable in their prices considering the difficulty and distance of transportation. We rode to the river, and Anderson and myself crossed, leaving our horses with Burgett. The fording was crowded with emigrants and we had to wait nearly an hour for an opportunity of getting a passage across. We had been informed that the village was only one-half mile from the river; but actually found it about two miles, and a bad road. Having had no dinner, and being wet from a rain that had fallen in a heavy shower, we began to feel the demands of appetite as night approached, and we had yet to cross the river, and travel on to camp. We were detained again in returning, and found it sundown when we got over. We found Burgett who had kept our horses, at his post though well drenched with rain, chilly and hungry, with ourselves. We moved briskly towards camp and got in about 10 o'clock at night.

MAY 13. — Rose early, and marched twelve miles to a small lake through which runs a beautiful creek of clear good water, where we encamped until the 15th, making some alteration in the arrangement of our loading, recruiting our oxen and preparing ourselves for the fatigues of the journey still before us. We were up by daylight on the morning of the 15th, being Monday, and ready for marching; but were detained an hour or two by a heavy thunder gust, after which we travelled eighteen miles, and encamped about 6 o'clock in the evening.

MAY 16. — Were on the road at 5 o'clock in the morning, and marched regularly all day; made twenty miles, and encamped within a mile of the Big Vermillion river, on the borders of a small stream, having crossed several small creeks during the day, the largest of which was the small Vermillion. We crossed the big Vermillion on the morning of the 17th, and travelled fifteen miles to big Blue River, by four o'clock in the afternoon. This river is generally fordable, except after heavy rains. There is no ferry, and all emigrants think themselves fortunate when it is fordable; when indeed it is practicable in any way to cross over its waters. We, by a kind providence, found it in a fordable condition; but could not have driven through it, had the water been a few inches higher. The water came up to some of our wagon beds, and had it been a little higher would no doubt have injured our provisions. We encamped immediately after crossing the river, and a small tributary running into it near the fording, where we had excellent grass, wood and water; the three great essential elements of good camp ground. The water of this small river is clear and pleasant and abounding with fish of the best quality.

Having eighteen miles to make on our way, before reaching a good place for encampment, we were up by day-light and on the road which presented through the day a scene eliciting the astonishment of the most sanguine, on the subject of western emigration. For several hours an almost unbroken train of wagons were wending their way over the vast plains towards the far west. It resembled some grand procession, and was calculated to suggest grave reflections on the probable results of such a mighty impulse of humanity toward these new and extreme borders of the American continent. Some out of such a large number may never reach the point of their destination, and the grave of an emigrant with an humble inscription on a board, rendered the conjecture to which we have referred, a positive certainty. He was interred near the road on a rising spot; his name was Benjamin Adams. Near the Blue River we passed the graves of two, under a large spreading oak; which had been barked, and their inscription cut on the tree; one was an old woman of seventy, Sarah Keyes, from Illinois, who had died the 29th of May, 1846, emigrating at that advanced age, and at so early a period of Western Emigration. The other's name was John Fuller, who had been accidentally shot on the 29th of April, 1849. Society is so dear to man, that even to see the grave of a departed one in the wide, uninhabited plan or desert, suggests solitary feelings and instinctively excites that feeling so common to all, a desire to sleep with our fathers.

Destiny in almost every shade must mark the history of such a vast multitude moving to a new far distant and in many respects destitute country. But our people are rightly characterized for enterprize, and despite of distance and danger, the most remote point in our country has only to develop its hidden resources, to secure a population. Encamped about five o'clock, near a pond of indifferent water, without any wood but a small stick from our wagons.

The next morning we rose and left before daylight. Travelled five miles to the head of a small putrid stream, where we took breakfast, and grazed our oxen a couple of hours; passed a creek of tolerable water, and encamped in the evening by a pond of stagnant water, that was our only supply except a little we had brought from a creek, which we had passed during the day. Passed the graves of two emigrants to-day, Landon, from Ohio, and McClelland, from Kentucky; the former had died of typhoid fever; the latter had been accidentally killed by his mule team taking fright and running off.

The surface of the country in the neighborhood of the big Blue River is considerably broken and hilly, but had now become more level. The streams were now stagnant and scarce; but few of them indeed had any current whatever. And

15

many of them were nothing more than marshy ponds which from appearances, dried up entirely in the summer season. Most of the emigrants had vessels to carry water; but we unfortunately had procured none, and now began to feel their want.

MAY 19. — Travelled five miles to little Sandy Creek, where we found a good encampment, and as it was now Saturday we concluded to remain here and rest on the holy Sabbath according to the commandment. The stream no doubt takes its name from the great amount of sand along the shore, which we found becoming common to all the streams we had crossed for some days. At the point where the road crossed this stream; we found considerable of a hill involving both sides of the Creek. The northwest side where we encamped, presented a beautiful scenery. The plain was variegated with hills and bluffs; a shade of timber marked the course of the creek running out on the side we occupied, much like an old orchard. We fancied that the trees were in rows; some certainly were. They were a species of oak, with low, round spreading tops like the apple tree. At the bottom of the hill, we discovered a fine spring of water quite a luxury to the thirsty traveller, and in the Creek passing by, we caught some small fish which were excellent.

MONDAY, MAY 21. — Were on the road at sunrise. The weather was cool and fine for travelling, and having made twenty miles, we encamped within a few miles of the Tuckapaw River, on a branch of the same. Saw to-day, a number of Buffalo skulls and Elk horns along the road, facts rather agreeable and suggestive as indications of our approach to game. Already we had become very tired of salt meat and cheering indeed were now the prospects of a change. We had a full stock of provisions, but unfortunately not much variety, nor such as we knew now were best adapted to keep up our constitutional vigor with the elements of ordinary health. Our stock consisted mainly of crackers, mess pork, and some groceries; without ham, milk, dried meal, molasses, &c., that should always be included in a stock of provisions for the route. A milk cow for ten men would be a great advantage, and attended with but little trouble.

MAY 22. — Were on march early, and travelled twenty miles up the Tuckapaw. The road was excellent, except a few places crossing and rounding some hollows or ravines, emptying into the stream. They were entirely dry, but as it is in oriental countries, they appeared to have been the channels of streams of a former period of time. The shades of evening now gather around us, and with not a discordant note to disturb the harmony of our intentions, we encamp for the night on the bank of the river, selecting an elevated and beautiful point, near which we discovered a fountain of the natural beverage so welcome to the thirsty and weary traveller.

After leaving camp in the morning we met Mr. Loft, one of our original company, on horseback, and was sorry to learn that Daniel O'Conner, another of our first company had accidentally shot himself on the day before, while unloading some things from a wagon. He was an Irishman about 40 years of age, leaving no family I believe, to mourn over his death. This solemn event forcibly impressed us all. Loft, our friend on horseback, with the conviction that he had already seen the elephant, set his face forthwith towards his home in the States.

MAY 23. — Left early and proceeded up the Tuckapaw twenty miles. We encamped in the evening close by the river, on the other side of which was a dense thicket of timber and bushes for some rods in extent. During the night while Mr. Hains, was on guard, and when but a few steps from the camp, he was alarmed by the crack of a rifle near at hand, and immediately informed those asleep, most of whom indeed had been awakened by the noise or report of the fire arms in question. After some lookout for the source of this alarm, we retired until the light of the morning might lead to some discovery. And now in the light of the morning sun, it is ascertained that a rifle ball had passed through the crown of the watchman's hat — scarcely missing his head — . We supposed it to have come from an Indian rifle across the river, from the thicket on the other side, and in the future were ever careful to select encampments offering better security from random shots fired by the Indians.

MAY 24th. — After a few miles' travel we left the bank of the stream on which we had been travelling for over fifty miles, and took a more westerly course towards Platte River. This river is twenty miles distant from the point where the road leaves the Tuckapaw, or Republican Fork. The day was cool and cloudy with intervals of sunshine, and towards evening indicated a general rain; the rain had already commenced in the evening when we encamped for the night, without any water but a small pond, and without any wood but staves, &c., from our wagons. Our coffee that night received no praise from any one of the company; whether its indifferent quality was attributable to the quality of the water, or the scarcity of wood or both together, was too abstract a question for the calm, dispassionate consideration of ten hungry, wet and tired men; and a gentle hint that the cook was in fault at once settled the question. Our cattle had been unyoked and turned on the Prairie to graze as usual. While the rain however, increased with a violent wind, they had wandered far over the plain, when the time arrived to bring them in and secure them for the night. This we did by tying them to the wagons. Scattered as they were far over the plain, we were successful in bringing them together and securing them for the night after which we retired to our tents where we had always heretofore enjoyed entire security from the heaviest rain that had fallen upon us; especially when we had adopted the process of trenching to carry away the water. But we now occupy an elevated spot, and the rain being accompanied by a hurricane of wind, we soon found our tent overflowing with water. We trenched it inside, which failing also, we were driven to our wagons for shelter. Those were so

17

well filled up with other commodities, that we, well-soaked specimens of humanity, had but little room and poor accommodations.

MAY 25. — Weather very cold, and wind very strong. After last night's extremely severe storm, we travelled twelve miles to the Platte River and encamped.

CHAPTER THREE

Journey along the Platte to the borders of the Sweetwater River.

MAY 26.—Having arrived at the Platte River, we proceeded along its banks in an upward direction for about ten miles, and encamped a little below Fort Kearny, where we improved an opportunity of writing to our friends. The Fort was but lately established; no buildings were yet up, but those built of sward taken from the surface of the Prairie. About one hundred soldiers were on the ground, and actual preparations were in a state of energetic prosecution for the erection of a garrison and other buildings necessary for the regular military fortification of the place. Here we found a small store, but as the demand for goods had been greater than the supply, the prices were very high, and even at the most exorbitant rates, the stock had been almost exhausted, being bought out by needy emigrants. To take the advantage of a fellow creature's necessity, is a developement [*sic*] of human nature, found even here in the wilderness.

MAY 27.—Travelled 12 miles, and encamped in a small slough, or swell running into the Platte. We found indeed a number of such creeks emptying into the Platte, but all appear to dry up in the summer season, as their channels are generally grown up with grass. We had adopted a resolution and practically followed it heretofore, to lay up on the Sabbath, but a number of circumstances, induced us to regard it as justifiable to make a short march to-day.

MAY 28.—Rose early and travelled fifteen miles to the Platte River valley; one of the most beautiful in the world, extending on each side of the River for several miles in an unbroken plain, covered at this season of the year with a rich growth of Prairie grass; a slight bluff ridge rises some miles from the River beyond which, it again becomes level. The River is nearly as wide as the Mississippi, and would appear navigable from sight, but is quite shallow and has no regular channel, the bottom being sand principally, and the whole body of the River dotted with little Islands, furnishing nearly all the timber and bushes to be seen as we pass along its green and fertile banks. It has more the appearance a grand canal passing through a level country, instead of being a River or what its name indicates. Its water is very muddy, and abounds with fish. Game is also very plenty in its vicinity, such as Deer, Antelope, &c., and traces of Buffalo have been recognized so as to render their proximity to our pathway beyond all reasonable doubt. Some of our company took a hunt today, but with no better success than to see a large number of Antelopes.

MAY 29. — Travelled twenty miles up the Platte. The road was good and the grass much better than where we first struck the River. We were in a large train all day composed of various companies that had happened to come together, having encamped together, about 4 o'clock along the valley, the united trains presented more the appearance of a great army than a few lonely emigrants. There came up a severe thunder gust in the night, with a heavy rain which continued late the next morning, and rendered it difficult with our scant stock of fuel to prepare breakfast.

MAY 30. — Left camp late in consequence of bad weather. — Roads heavy all day; — wind very high and cold. Encamped early, having travelled about twelve miles.

MAY 31. — The weather cloudy and cold with a drizzling rain that continued most of the day. As our oxen were fatigued, and wet weather unfavorable at any time for driving, we lay up to-day making ourselves as comfortable as possible under the circumstances of discomfort in which we were placed. In the evening we readjusted our loads by sacrificing several barrels of crackers, and throwing away the barrels, together with all our boxes and chests that we could dispense with. This we found necessary, to reduce our loads, which were several hundred pounds too heavy for our teams, especially on a long journey. Others had learned the same lesson by a few week's experience, and numerous articles might be seen strewed along the road that had been thrown out to lighten the wagons; in some cases even provisions were thrown away.

JUNE 1. — Rose early and were pursuing the long but beautiful road up the Platte as soon as our train could be fairly set in motion. The inclement weather seemed to have passed away, but the roads were heavy in consequence of the recent rains. — Travelled fifteen miles and encamped immediately on the bank of the river. The sun set clear, and the green valley washed by a beautiful river dotted with small Islands and shaded by a few scattering trees, along its shore presented a view so enchanting, so full of sublimity as fully to indemnify us for the fatigues of the day.

JUNE 2. — Were on the road early, the weather fine, and the roads much improved. And having travelled twenty miles, we encamped on Rapid Creek emptying into the river. Its head we ascertained was only a few miles up the river in a large slew, or pond. It was the only stream we had found emptying into the Platte thus far. It was a place of general camping. From our own camp we could see a number of others around, and as the moon shone on the vast green plain, the tents and herds spread out on its face reminded us of the ancient and patriarchal or pastoral life so beautifully described amid the recorded facts of Bible history. —

Early the next morning we were aroused at daylight by the report of Buffalo! Buffalo! that echoed from camp to camp. And soon the plain was covered with men in close pursuit of a small drove of Buffalo that had crossed the river in the night and had come among the encampments: A few were fortunate enough to be mounted on horses; a providential arrangement soon found to be necessary in a Buffalo chase. Most of us were new hands at the business; but succeeded admirably withal as five or six of the denizens of the plain were shot down, affording an ample supply for all the camps represented in the chase, and a surplus for others that passed during the day. We had been confined to salt meat for several weeks; and were prepared to do ample justice to a dish of steak — being unanimous in our verdict that the meat was excellent. We salted a small quantity for the future, not knowing how to jerk it as is usually done. Each one of our company had been ambitious of shooting the first Buffalo; an honor assigned to L.A. Ream who had captured and killed a choice member of the flock early in the morning.

JUNE 4. — Rose early, and pursued the road up the Platte till about noon, when we were under the necessity of crossing. With some other trains we went below the usual fording and crossed. The river was wide, rapid and muddy, but fortunately for us was now in a fordable state. The south fork at the point where we forded it was nearly a mile wide, and looked somewhat dangerous but it is very shallow in proportion to the distance across it, and except when swollen from heavy rains, or melting snows at its head in the mountains, can be forded always with comparative safety. We doubled our teams in crossing; which made for them several trips across instead of one. However we all got over safely about 4 o'clock in the evening, and immediately went into camp, to avail ourselves of dry clothes, and fire to counteract the effects of the wet and cold. We had with us a small quantity of Brandy for medicinal purposes; and as such phraseology includes prevention as well as cure; we concluded that now was the proper occasion for its use, and accordingly our physician Dr. Marshall, prescribed in the case, and having prepared the medicine in his best professional style, administered it to us individually and collectively when around our camp fires for the night.

JUNE 5. — Left early and marched up the south fork for a few miles over a newly marked road, and then bore towards the north fork which we reached in a few miles, and kept on it during the day travelling about twenty miles. We had met some Indians before crossing, but found them quite numerous in the forks, and during the forenoon before leaving the south fork, passed an Indian village of over a hundred huts or tents made with tanned Buffalo skins sewed together, and supported by reeds or poles. They came out en masse to see us pass their town, and appeared pleased to see us. But before we had run the gauntlet of their scrutinizing and curious gaze, we judged their attentions to originate more in selfishness than benevolent sympathy. It was evidently more on account of our loaves and fishes than from any feelings of sympathetic friendship in our behalf. It was a heavy tax indeed which they were inclined to levy, in their numerous applications for food and other presents. We gave them a few articles which they seemed particularly to covet, effected some small trades and proceeded on our way without molestation. But the shades of the evening have come—and we encamp for the night.

JUNE 6.—Left early and proceeded up this branch of the river several miles, when we left the valley, ascended the bluff or second bank and travelled the remainder of the day on a high rolling plain, coming to the fork again in the evening through a deep ravine of a sandy and dry bottom. About noon a heavy thunder storm accompanied with hail, came up so suddenly that we had scarcely time to turn our cattle out on the prairie, and seek the protection of our wagons, our only shelter at such times, before the tornado spent its violence over and around us. The sun shone out in the evening, and the plain seemed to wear a deeper green from the refreshing influence of the recent rain. Encamped on the fork at five o'clock.

JUNE 7.—Left camp at 6 o'clock and travelled eighteen miles, still up the north fork of the river Platte. As the valley had become narrow in places we were obliged every few miles to ascend the bluff and travel on the high plain, which though rolling and sometimes hilly; was not so much so as to prevent us from driving safely and with tolerable speed. We had now travelled about a month with a company of ten men, or rather thirteen, as three others with a wagon had fallen in our train, and travelled with us, and three young gentlemen from the vicinity of Massillon, Ohio. As a guard at night is indispensable on the route, we began to find it a serious inconvenience to be called out on duty as often as our small number required. And accordingly we made application to a train of twenty wagons and sixty men, consisting of the company from Ashland, O., and a small company from Illinois, to travel and encamp with them, a proposition to which we met a prompt and cordial compliance and in accordance with this new arrangement, we all encamped together in the evening. It was an earlier hour than usual when we stopped, having come to an excellent spring of water at the base of the river bluff, around which were also a few scattering ash and cedar trees, apparently in their origin designed for ornament, but were now transferred to the opposite scale of utility in the way of replenishing our reduced stock of fuel. An encampment on this route affording good wood and water is emphatically an "Oasis," in the desert where the emigrant after having quenched his thirst for days or weeks on pond or river water, and carefully economizing his little supply of wood, he can now enjoy the luxury of water cold and fresh from the fountain, and hasten the preparation of his meal by a liberal supply of wood from the forest.

JUNE 8.—Having stopped early the previous day we were prepared for an early start this morning. Rose at three o'clock, and left camp at five, ascended a steep Bluff, and travelled a few miles over a rolling plain; when we gradually wound into a deep ravine that soon gave unmistakeable proof from the ash trees scattered along its course that we were in "Ash hollow," a point well known to all travelers on this road and marked on all its charts.

It is three or four miles in length, abounding with large and beautiful ash trees, together with some other varieties of timber and bushes. The wild rose and other flowers decorated the place with their gayest colors, and lent their sweetest perfume to the balmy gale. A crystal stream flowed from a deep recess at the base of the bluff that overlooked the green little vale below. We travelled leisurely through this attractive spot; and felt more pain than pleasure, when we emerged from its delightful shades and found ourselves again on the monotonous valley pursuing our course up the North Branch of the Platte. We found sandy roads a great part of the day, which rendered our progress onward, sometimes difficult in the extreme. Not being able to obtain grass for our cattle at the usual hour of encampment, it was late in the evening before we could make our arrangements for the desirable repose of the night.

The next morning June 9th, being wet we remained in the camp until eight o'clock, found sandy and difficult roads part of the day, and were obliged to ascend the bluff several times which greatly impeded our progressive operations. Travelled fifteen miles and encamped at five o'clock in the evening.

JUNE 10. — This is the holy sabbath, and in accordance with our custom we observe the day. We cease from our marching, and some of us I trust, as individuals, try to rest in the fear and worship of the Lord. And although cut off from the house of God, and deprived of many precious privileges enjoyed at home, yet some of us fully appreciated and enjoyed this sabbath in the wilderness.

JUNE 11th. — Rose at three o'clock, and were on march soon after sun rise. A heavy rain had fallen the previous night which rendered the roads heavy and difficult to travel during the day. Made sixteen miles and encamped opposite Court House Rock, which had been visible for hours, and furnished an object of curiosity for all. We thought it only two or three miles off, and calculated to visit it after supper; when one of our men came in on horseback and informed us they had been two hours traveling from the Rock to our Camp; our purpose was of course abandoned. It is so called from its resemblance at a distance, to a large Court House. It is 250 feet high; and when approached presents a rough, high mass, of a species of limestone and sand.

JUNE 12th. — Left camp at five o'clock; travelled fifteen miles — encamping opposite Chimney Rock, which was in view from the previous day. It rises in a regular conical form, being about 300 yards in circumference at its base, and about 200 feet high; runing [sic] gradually to a point on the top till within 40 or 50 feet of the pinnacle, when a round column of stone some 80 or 100 feet in diameter, of a soft texture apparently part lime, and part sand; stands

23

perpendicular on the top. Supposing it only a small walk a number hastened off to visit it, and a cedar hollow near it while supper was being prepared, but like all other objects viewed at a distance on the plain, it proved much farther than we had anticipated.

A heavy rain had fallen during the evening which rendered it difficult to ascend, besides having eaten nothing since early in the morning, except lunch at noon, I contented myself with a view of it merely, not feeling the promptings of ambition sufficiently powerful under the circumstances to climb the rugged slippery steeps of this Rock and to engrave my name on its face, as hundreds have done before. A few drenching rains totally obliterates the engraving. *"Sic transit gloria mundi."* "So fades the glory of the world." How many votaries of Ambition in the history of time have sacrificed health, principle, friends, and even life itself, to make their mark on this rock of fame. But how soon does the mark disappear amid the oblivious sands of this fleeting existence.

JUNE 13th. — Rose at three, and were on the march at five o'clock left the Platte fork in the forenoon, and bore westerly through a beautiful valley of a few miles in width, bordered with high, rugged bluffs; which were adorned with scattering and beautiful Cedar trees. Having found no water at our usual hour for encampment we were under the necessity of driving till six o'clock P.M., when we found a scant supply, and turned in for the night after a day's journey of 22 miles.

JUNE 14th. — We were on march early; crossed a deep ravine in the forenoon with a small stream of water in its bed, which came from a pure spring half a mile above, around which was a dense thicket of bushes, vines, cedars and other shrubbery, with all the beauty of natural deformity, and with all the order of natural confusion.

The imagination of the traveler can detect in the very deformities of nature many elements of beauty; and in the wild disorder of hill and forest, and the sandy plain the established order of nature's great Architect; the Lord Jehovah himself.

But my thirst clips the wings of my imagination; and now for the fountain of water at the head of this ravine. We ascended its bank weary to the spring before crossing the ravine; and this afforded an excellent opportunity to replenish our water canteens, which had been empty for some time. Crossed Horse Shoe creek in the afternoon, and encamped a few miles beyond it. Here we found a well affording good water for our own use, and a pond of water for our cattle.

Water can be had by digging from 5 to 8 feet, almost any place in the valley of the Platte, although the surface of the soil is dry and sandy, and very unpromising in reference to this great element of life. As a number of wells had been dug by those in advance of us, we availed ourselves of their use — finding them a great convenience — a happy providential arrangement in our behalf.

JUNE 15. — Left camp at 6 o'clock, and proceeded up the valley in which we travelled yesterday, for several miles, when we again struck the fork of the Platte. Passed a train of wagons belonging to the United States, with an escort of soldiers going to Ft. Larimie, with provisions for that important establishment. We encamped in the same neighborhood for the night, having travelled, perhaps, more than 20 miles.

JUNE 16. — Left camp at our usual time, and proceeded about 12 miles to Ft. Larimie [sic] branch, a narrow deep rapid stream, that proved more difficult to cross than the South fork itself. In fording this stream, we were subjected to the same difficulty experienced on the part of others before us. We were obliged to raise our wagon beds with blocks, so inserted as to give them the proper elevation, from being carried away by the water. We got over safely, except one wagon containing crackers, that got slightly damaged by coming in contact with the water, or rather by being immersed in it. Ft. Larimie is situated on this stream — a branch emptying into the North fork of the Platte. It is handsomely situated in a circular valley — surrounded at some distance by a regular circular bluff, with the stream we crossed, passing close by its east side, and furnishing an abundant supply of water.

It is 60 or 70 feet square, with a wall 10 feet high, and nearly as broad, composed of prairie sward, which here contains a large quantity of sand, and appears to have become hard and durable. There are numerous rooms neatly fitted up for the officers and soldiers, and from a point in the wall, our national flag waves high, inspiring the weary emigrant with new emotions of patriotic regard for the land of his birth; a country that even in these western wildes, [sic] has planted her colors, and made provision for the security of her citizens. We look at this banner floating above us — the generous eagle points to the pathway of Republican Empire, and the propitious stars shoot a gladdening ray.

"Star spangled Banner, long may it wave,
O'er the land of the free and the home of the brave!"

We halted an hour at the fort, examining its varrious [sic] apartments, and indulging in the strange curiosity of gazing upon a habitation involving the signs and some of the things signified, pertaining to man's civilized state. But at the same time this Fort with its munitions of war, involves a fact not very complimentary to our civilization, that the rights of the poor Indian have been so invaded, and his combative passions so aroused in consequence of the encroachment, as to create a necessity for this defensive establishment on the great highway to the Pacific shores. This indeed was the only abode, reminding us of a comfortable home in the States, the only one that we had seen for weeks. — Hence we proceeded up the Larimie branch a mile or two, and ascended a high bluff, bearing South West for 6 or 7 miles where we encamped one mile from water, and very inferior grain for our poor cattle.

25

JUNE 17. — The Lord's day is again with us. It is one of our rules not to desecrate it. We wish to do as the Israelites did in the wilderness of Sinai, to keep the Sabbath as a day, holy unto the Lord. But having no miraculous provision for ourselves and our oxen, it becomes a matter of necessity and mercy now, to move a little in advance, on the morning of this sacred day. Marched 6 miles over hilly, dry and sandy roads, when we reached a large spring some few rods north east of our road, where we stopped a couple of hours, watering our cattle and replenishing our exhausted water vessels. The water was clear and sweet but remarkably warm. A large circle however was formed around it drinking copiously of its waters. But with plenty of water now, what will we do with our starving cattle? We look around and see no grass; the poor animals have nothing to eat. Pressed by the necessity of the case, we advanced 5 miles further; passing up a deep ravine, and ascending a steep hill on to a high and rolling plain, from which the surrounding bluffs and hills presented a more high and rugged, and irregular apparance than usual; evidently indicating our approach to the black hills or suburbs of the Rocky mountains. Found tolerable forage about three o'clock, where we encamped, without any water, except that brought with us in our kegs and canteens, and other vessels with the proper qualifications for transporting this precious liquor of God's creation.

JUNE 18. — Rose at three o'clock, and travelled six miles to Heber Spring, before breakfasting, where we found abundance of wood, and a noble spring of clear cold water. It might almost be called a little lake — being several rods in circumference and from 5 to 6 feet deep. We pitched our tents here for the day as other emigrant trains are accustomed to do, with a view to recruit their animals, and enjoy the luxury of the spring, and the shade of the surrounding trees.

JUNE 19. — Left camp at 5 o'clock, and marched 15 miles, over a rough hilly road. Finding scarcely sufficient water for our cattle, at a small spring about noon. Encamped on Horse Shoe creek in the evening, where we had an excellent spring. On the morning of the 20th, we were on the march at an early hour, and after having travelled 18 miles of a road, if possible, more rough and difficult for our teams than that of the previous day; we encamped on the Levant, a large creek of clear good water, with abundance of wood along its shore, but the provender for our cattle very inferior indeed.

JUNE 21. — Started early and made our usual day's journey of 16 - 18 miles, over roads, bad no doubt, from their earliest origin, and by no means improved by the lapse of time or the current of emigration. The day was extremely warm, and the cattle as well as ourselves, were overcome with weariness, and with an evident tendency of exhaustion, when we encamped.

JUNE 22. — Rose at 2 o'clock and travelled 8 miles to a place where we had wood water and tolerable grass. Here we laid up till the afternoon, when we left for Deer creek, a branch of the North fork of the Platte, which we again struck in the afternoon, after 80 miles' travel over exceedingly bad roads, being hilly, rough and sandy, and dusty in the extreme; and this scarcely without an exception, since we lost sight of the Platte river, and grass very scarce, and water only in the neighborhood of the creeks, which we found to be 12 or 20 miles apart. But while we had for a short time lost sight of this river, taking a shorter course through the hills, we were still ascending the stream itself. We are still on our journey up the Platte river, on to the Sweetwater.

JUNE 23. — Remained in camp to-day, enjoying the luxuriant shade, afforded by the beautiful grove of poplar, along the banks of the creek. This creek abounds in excellent fish, and with the prerogative extended in the covenant of old, we appropriated an adequate supply of these inhabitants of the water, to supply our immediate wants. On the next morning we went up this fork of the Platte two miles, to the point where we had made arrangements to cross. This branch of the Platte is narrower and deeper than the South fork. It runs with great rapidity, and is from 4 and 5 to 10 feet in depth. The Mormons have established a ferry a few miles above Deer Creek. But we bought a boat constructed of several canoes, lashed and pinned together. With some plank laid upon them, a wagon with a light load, could be taken over by this boat. It had been built by some of the first emigrants, sold to others and then again sold to others with no diminution of the original price, till it came into our hands. We paid $40 for it, and when done with it, sold it immediately for the same. This was a fine stroke of ecomony, as the Mormons charged three dollars per wagon for their services. What may ultimately become of that boat, I know not, but whatever may be its future destiny, it has been useful in its day and generation, an affirmation that cannot be made of all the rational beings that passed over this river in this frail canoe vessel.

We put over a few wagons on the evening of the 24th, and had all taken over and marched a few miles on the 25th. But while our teams were all taken over in safety, we met, nevertheless, with a calamity on the morning of this 25th of June, which cast over us a deep gloom, and touched the most sensitive chord of our nature — Daniel Burgett, one of our company from Stark county, Ohio, while attempting to swim his horse across, by some means got disengaged from the animal, and in attempting to swim to shore, was swept down the rapid current and sank to rise no more. He was a young man of superior intelligence and integrity; much esteemed by the company, and deeply regretted by all. During the day, we made dilligent search for the body, but in vain. — The current is deep and swift and the bottom a bed of sand. The body was therefore, liable to be carried rapidly down the stream, or soon to be buried in the sand. Informed as we were, that several had been drowned at this very point, and none found after the most long continued search. We abandoned the search reluctantly; a search that would not have been relinquished for days, had there been any reasonable hope of success. We left the place with heavy hearts, our evening meal was taken in silence, and a sadness marked our little circle as we sat around our camp fire, like that of a family which had lost a beloved member.

JUNE 26. — Travelled 20 miles up the North fork, and on the morning of the 27th, left camp early and marched 35 miles over a barren country and sandy road. After going 10 or 15 miles, we left the North fork, and found no water till late in the evening, but that which was so strongly tinctured with alkali as to be dangerous even for cattle. And the demonstration of this fact we had in the number of dead cattle strewed along our road. — Encamped at Willow Springs, which are cold and agreeable, but highly charged with sulphur. As the most of the trains in advance of us had been accustomed to make this a camping place, no grass was left for our cattle. And by daylight on the morning of the 28th, we left this Willow Spring encampment, and having proceeded 7 or 8 miles, we rested several hours to graze our cattle, and to refresh ourselves with as good a breakfast as we could procure, or scare up under the circumstances. Afterwards travelled on till late in the evening, making twenty miles. Were obliged to go two or three miles off the road for grass. One of our men, (Haines), happened to sit down and fall asleep as we were leaving the road; when he awoke, he supposed we were still on the road in advance of him, and made rapid steps to reach his friends on the wrong track. We were anxious about his destiny during the night; but our apprehensions proved unfounded. The man was safe. The wings of a particular providence had been over him, and we found him safe the next morning, in an advanced train.

CHAPTER FOUR

Journey from the Sweetwater, by the way of Fort Bridger, to Salt Lake City.

UNE 29.—After travelling 12 miles, we struck the Sweetwater River—a small but handsome stream. Passed Independence Rock, which stands near both the river and the road. It stands out in the bottom of the valley—detached from the point of the mountain near; it is a huge mass of granite rock—rather regular in its general outlines, and rounding on the top. Its base covers several acres, and it is said to be 250 feet high. Hundreds have engraven [*sic*] their names in the most prominent places.— Some are cut in the Rock—while others, less ambitious, or less willing to take the trouble, have contented themselves with merely writing in characters formed by the use of tar, or some corresponding material, that only makes a transitory impression.

We passed up Sweetwater 8 miles, and encamped near a deep cut through a mountain called "Devil's Gate." The river appears to have run round the mountain point formerly, and found its way here through a large crevice, which has gradually crumbled down and washed away until the cut is clear to the top of the mountain. It is three or four hundred feet deep, and nearly perpendicular. The river dashes through like a cataract over the rocks that have fallen in its channel. A person can get through along the shore, but with considerable difficulty as well as danger. And here I can give the testimony of my own experience, that whoever undergoes the fatigue of walking through that cut once, will feel but little curiosity to pass through again.

JUNE 30th.—Travelled up Sweetwater 20 miles, and encamped until July 2nd. The 1st was the Sabbath. Welcome, even here in the wilderness; "welcome sweet day of rest that saw the Lord arise." We laid by on this sacred day. We had water from the river and tolerable grass; our only resort for fuel being the "Wild Sage" or "Artemesia," as it is scientifically or technically called. Four of the train with which we travelled left on horseback this morning to go on in advance of the train, and make arrangements as far as possible for quarters immediately on its arrival. The men were Patterson, White, Luther and Woods. Travelled 20 miles over roads generally level—but very sandy and dusty, rendering it exceedingly disagreeable to those driving the teams.— Crossed the river three times, within a

29

few hours of the afternoon. The scenery often blended the wild, the beautiful and sublime; the mountain tops on opposite sides of the stream sometimes appearing to join together as though identified in fond embrace. — Encamped a short distance from the river, in a beautiful high valley. We appeared surrounded by mountains as a wall; and from their summit we could distinctly see the snow, where it had drifted in deep ravines and crevices, and hollows, formed by the rocks in their wild and careless order.

JULY 3d. — Our cattle being very much fatigued, we concluded this morning to lay up, and re-arrange our goods, &c. — dispensing with every thing that we possibly could to lighten our wagons for the oxen. To effect this object, we divided our stock into three shares or messes, or rather into individual shares, and afterwards formed three messes. Rudy and Ream formed one mess, McConnel and myself another, and our remaining companion the third mess in question. I had bought out Dr. Marshall's interest; and now, as they sometimes throw goods overboard into the Ocean to save the vessel, we were compelled to make a similar sacrifice. Whatever may be our future necessities — we now throw away bread and pork — and various other articles that must be sacrificed in order to advance at all. Having completed our new arrangement, we drove five miles in the evening.

JULY 4th. — We had intended for weeks to stop and celebrate the day; but some having gone on in advance, the first of the month, and we being compelled to stop the day before, were several miles behind our train, without any certainty that they would stop for the desired celebration. We started early hoping to find them in a few hours, but travelled hard till in the afternoon, some 3 or 4 o'clock, when we came up to a train from Springfield, Illinois, with some of our original company. They were just closing the exercises of the celebration, and we dispairing of a patriotic manifestation with our own train, resolved to join our Illinois friends in their celebration — sharing in the sequel of their performances an excellent dish of wild ducks.

JULY 5th. — Left the camp at 5 o'clock in the morning, and reached Willow Creek before our evening encampment — having travelled 18 miles over rough roads. One of our teams, belonging to Ream and Rudy, went on a few miles further with the view of overtaking the train. We encamped on the bank of the creek, turned our cattle out in the bottom, and after a cup of tea and some crackers, retired for the night, without either a guard or tying our cattle, — quite a risk indeed, and contrary to an invariable rule. A kind providence, however, watched over us and preserved us in safety. We slept undisturbed, and found our cattle together in the morning.

JULY 6th. — Were on the road early, and reached the Summit Springs, at the western end of the South Pass, making 18 miles. — The roads to-day were much better than we anticipated; being tolerably level with gradual ascents and descents. The pass presents the appearance of a high rolling plain or prairie, from 20 to 50 miles in width, walled on each side by high and broken mountain cliffs, covered with snow, which seemed to be yielding gradually to the heat of the Sun on the south side, and the swollen and muddy developments of the streams indicated a supply of water from that source—no rain of any account having fallen since we left the Platte River, below Fort Larimie. And since we left that place nearly a month has elapsed. Now, in reference to these mountain snows, what a source of supply they must be during the dry season, in the absance [*sic*] of the refreshing rains of Heaven. — Truly the provisions of nature are mysterious; but they are infinitely bountiful and wise. The laws of nature are the laws of God.

JULY 7th. — Left camp at 3 o'clock, intending to travel a few miles before breakfast, as we had to travel 22 miles before reaching a good camping place for the night; but took no water with us, and found none for nine miles. A small stream, called Dry Sandy, crossed the road; but we unfortunately found it so brackish and bitter that we could not use it. We drove over it a mile or two and rested our cattle a couple of hours, taking both a cold and dry check for breakfast, after which we resumed our march. The wind blew extremely high, and coming from the west against us, and the road being very deep with dust and sand, it was difficult to proceed at all; but stern necessity compelled us, and we proceeded through to Little Sandy, where we arrived about 3 o'clock, and encamped. We hastened to prepare a meal which we hesitated to call breakfast, dinner or supper, as it combined all three for that day. Here we found but little grass, but abundance of wood and water. The Wild Sage is the only substitute for wood from the Platte River, and reference is always made to it when wood is mentioned on this point of the route. It grows to nearly the size of the Laurel, and in such abundance that it forms, to a great extent, the staple native production from Fort Larimie. The old dry stalks make a bright blazing fire, but soon burns up and is exhausted by the fury of its flames.

JULY 8th. — The holy Sabbath has again returned, and we welcomed it not only as a day of rest — but of religious reflection, and solemn devotional contemplation of the time, when our journey of life must end after its toils and trials, with the hope of spending our everlasting Sabbath in the "building not made with hands." In the evening, we drove down the Creek a few miles, where we found good grass for our cattle.

JULY 9. — Made an early start; crossed Big Sandy, after travelling ten miles, where we grazed and took dinner; afterwards proceeding with our teams till 4 o'clock; when the wind blew so strong, and the dust became so annoying, that we stopped a couple of hours, prepared supper, and again resumed the road at 6 o'clock, travelling on till about 9 o'clock. We concluded now to encamp, and took our position on a high bluff, in view of the Big Sandy, south east of the road, where we took our cattle to water at night and in the morning, nearly two miles distant.

JULY 10.—Were on the road early—crossed a small stream during the day, and reached Green river by 4 o'clock, eighteen miles, comprehending the distance of our locomotion during the day. We found the river too high to ford, and crossed in a boat. We found two ferries at this crossing. The one on which we crossed had been established a short time previous, in opposition to the other established by the Mormons, and had reduced the ferriage from $5 to $3 per wagon, which we paid, with the conviction that while competition is the life of trade, it does not always make bills with the bounds of reason. We got our wagons over before night, and attempted to swim our cattle, but after three unsuccessful efforts, left them till morning, when we took them higher up the river, and finally succeeded in getting them over.

JULY 11.—Being detained an hour longer than usual, did not get off before six o'clock, but made a hard day's drive. Went ten miles down the river, then leaving it fifteen miles, to Hamsfork, making twenty-five miles. And on the next morning, July 12th, left at 5 o'clock, our usual time; and having travelled eighteen miles, encamped on Black fork, where we drove our cattle over the stream and found good grass.

JULY 12.—Reached Ft. Bridger, eighteen miles from last encampment. We encamped below the fort, where driving our cattle across the stream we found excellent grass.

JULY 14.—Having driven one hundred miles already this week, which was considered a good week's work for ox teams, we concluded to lay up this and the following day, an allotment of time, including the holy sabbath. We accordingly drove a short distance along the Fort, and selected a camp ground, affording wood, water and grass, and enjoyed that luxury which the weary traveler on this route can only appreciate properly—the luxury of rest.

On yesterday and to-day, we had a slight sprinkle of rain from clouds both south and east of us—which is all we have had for a month. The road being sandy, had become deep with dry, fine dust, that almost covered the teams and concealed them from our view, as they advanced over it—disagreeable and injurious in the extreme both to the drivers and animals. With this exception, we found the road thus far on the mountains much better than we anticipated, being often level for miles and a gradual ascent and descent over bluffs that here an there marked the valley; a valley indeed which was rather a high rolling plain over which we crossed and which stretched out from 40 to 50 miles, extending to the base of the mountains. These mountains appeared to rise several hundred feet higher, and were covered with snow appearing to melt but slowly, and we judged might remain on the highest peaks during the entire year. Although the sun is warm, and sometimes almost scorching on the Dry Sandy Plain; yet the cool refreshing breeze from the mountains counteracts it to a great extent and renders the weather comfortable during the day, but cool at night.

JULY 16th. — Rose by daylight, and were on the road soon after Sun up, leaving the Fork to the left we bore to the right over a wide bluff. We crossed a small stream of cold water, and came into a rolling plain covered with good grass. Then we descended a steep hill into a beautiful bottom, watered by a stream of cold water, at the edge of which, near the road, was a small grove of beautiful tall Willow trees — where we grazed our cattle and refreshed ourselves with the best dinner we could procure. After this little interval of our travelling labors, we ascended a high ridge and passed over several miles of rough roads. Encamped at 5 o'clock on the ridge near the point of a mountain around which the road bears to the right or West. Went a mile down into a ravine for water; — found abundance to water our cattle as well as for domestic use. But we were disappointed with regard to our abundant supply of water when we ascertained its quality. It was not good water — too strongly impregnated with alkali for man or beast. But under the present circumstances, "beggars were not to be choosers." Here was the alternative, bad water or none. While eating our evening meal, three Indians galloped into the camp; and, after their usual savage efforts at the ceremony of civilized salutation, manifested the selfishness of their benevolent regards by emphatic indications that they wanted something to eat. This appeal to our generosity both flattered and softened us, — and handing over to the poor savages some meat and a few crackers, we realized the truth of the inspired announcement that it is more "blessed to give than to receive." These Indians belonged to the Snake Tribe.

JULY 17th. — Left early, and travelled 25 miles. The roads were rough and hilly in the forenoon, but smoother in the after part of the day, running down a narrow valley for several miles. — Encamped near an excellent spring of cold water, a few rods to the left of the road. Being overcome with thirst, we drank almost intemperately; had excellent grass, but no wood. After being in camp a short time, several Indians came in with large loads of Wild Sage for wood. Poor fellows! — they were hungry, — and with some element of an independent spirit — and with some rude indefinite conceptions of political economy in reference to demand and supply — and with some faint views of justice in rendering an equivalent for what they received — they brought us what we needed to cook our evening meal; and, giving them in return something of which to make a supper themselves, they departed to their own camp well pleased with their operation in trade. We learned that these peaceable Indians were accustomed to this kind of trade with the emigrants as they passed along. — Simple hearted children of nature! — sons of the forest! — you never read the divine injunction, "labor not for the meat that perisheth" — nor the effusion of a human poet: —

> "Man wants but little here below,
> Nor wants that little long."

Still your lives are certainly more in accordance with such principles of common sense than the lives of those civilized and nominally Christian slaves to avarice, ambition, and fashion with which the world abounds.

JULY 18th. — We were on our road at the usual hour; had rough roads most of the day, but made 20 miles, reaching the Weaver River, where we found a good camping ground. This river is small, but rapid, and some what difficult to ford with teams. — And on the 19th we marched about the same distance of the previous day over the hardest kind of roads. Crossed several streams, and some of them a number of times; encamped on Kenyon Creek, by a spring at the road side to the right. During the past few days, we have passed numerous springs of water issuing from the mountain side, which are the most welcome waymarks to the weary traveller.

JULY 20th. — Proceeded a few miles down Kenyon Creek — crossing it in the mean time more than a dozen of times, and in some places with considerable difficulty encountered in the crossing. Having left the Creek, we ascended a narrow ravine three miles, where we entered upon the ascent of the highest mountain that had, so far, risen in our pathway. The ascent was very steep, and tedious; and the descent difficult and precipitous sometimes to a dangerous extreme. The road had worn into a deep gutter, running down into a timbered ravine. The timber had been cut away, but the stumps still remained. These were large stumps; they were numerous and not far between, rendering it almost impossible to wind through them. There had been no rain of any account for weeks, and the dust was very deep and annoying. Drove a few miles after reaching the valley, which was narrow and rough; and encamped on Brown Creek, having travelled fifteen miles and now within fourteen of the Mormon City, in the valley of Salt Lake, the Southern part of which we had got a glimpse of to-day from the mountain.

JULY 21. — Drove to the city and encamped on its Western suburb. The road continued very rough on to its very entrance into the valley, where it again became smooth and level. Except the distant view of a small portion of this valley, obtained from the mountain referred to on the 20th, it is entirely excluded from view until emerging from the deep ravine through which the road leads into it, when it opens its beauty and attractiveness all at once to the eye: — a vast level plain surrounding by snow-capped mountains; but enjoying a fine temperature and teaming with vegetation — the great Salt Lake lying in view to the West and South of it. The Mormons emigrated to this valley in 1847, and now have hundreds of acres under cultivation and a city built covering an area of many acres, and containing a population of 5,000, which, we believe, is unparalleled in history. Several streams of pure cold water, from the mountain, run through the valley, affording an abundance of water. And a number of the smaller streams they have carried around and through the city by artificial channels to irrigate their gardens and furnish water for domestic use. The valley is forty miles wide, and something more in length. The Lake is 240 miles long, and of unequal width, averaging, perhaps, 40 or 50. It contains a number of Islands, on some of which large mountains rise, never yet completely explored, according to the declarations of some travellers. The soil is good. The higher portions of the valley require irrigation to produce the most luxuriant harvests of grain, and scarcity of timber is the only important want in the general resources and facilities for improvement and comfort. They get timber in the mountains, 15 or 20 miles off, for building and other purposes. Stone coal has been discovered and procured 70 miles distant from the city; but, from indications founded on scientific research, they expect to have it more convenient of access for all their citizens.

JULY 22. — Being Sabbath, I prepared to attend church at the Mormon Temple, which, as yet, is but a large shed — a kind of foreshadowing of what their temple will be which they design to erect. We were so unfortunate, however, as to loose our cattle in the tall grass rushes, which cost us a half day's excursion to bring them together. Attended church in the afternoon, and felt no ordinary pleasure in meeting with a civilized assembly for religious worship in the far Western wilds, especially after months without enjoying that privilege. But alas! to express my conviction fully in a few words, the whole exercises seemed a burlesque on preaching and religous worship in general. What delusion! what foolery! what a blending of the world the flesh and the devil with external demonstrations of devotion and reverence for the authority of Heaven!

JULY 23d. — Wishing to recruit our cattle a few days before resuming our journey, and the Mormon anniversary of their landing in the valley coming off on the 24th, we concluded to remain in our present camp for a few days, and enjoy the luxuries of the occasion as well as the advantage of gaining information from them respecting our future journey and prospects, as a number of them had been at the California mines.

JULY 24th. — Attended the exercises at the Mormon Temple, which consisted mostly of speeches and music, after which we sat down to a sumptuous dinner with about 5000 of their own number besides a number of strangers, all of whom were invited to partake. The scene was magnificent, in the Rocky mountains, 1000 miles from the borders of civilization, where, but a few years ago, the barbarious Indian reared his smoky wig-wam, and ate his buffalo lunch by a blazing fire in its centre, and whose war-whoops still echo from the mountain tops as he retires from the appearance of civilization, now appear cultivated fields, a ripening harvest and a large and growing city—the citizens of which have met to-day to commemorate their arrival here only two years ago. The temple or large shed was the main dining room, but, being open at the sides, a covering of boards and canvass was extended from each, until an area of nearly an acre was protected from the Sun, and thrown into a most delightful shade and ample room for all to sit down at once. The company formed a procession by wards and marched in, taking their seats at the tables in regular order, and all passed off in good style, and we unanimously agreed, in good taste.

CHAPTER FIVE

Journey from Salt Lake City to Pleasant Valley, on the borders of the gold mines.

ULY 25. — Drove up the valley 14 miles, and encamped near several settlements of Mormons; had a good camp, and procured milk, butter and cheese from the Mormon settlers, at reasonable rates. About three miles from the city, the road passes the boiling springs, and still nearer the city, are the warm sulphur springs both coming out of the base of the mountain, and from large streams that cross the valley, and empty into the lake. We had visited the latter several times to bathe, while lying by the city. They are about eighty degrees *fahrenheit*, highly impregnated with sulphur, but very clear and transparent. They have a beautiful bed of white gravel; and visitors as yet, bathe at the fountain head, where it is several feet wide and two or three in depth. An extensive bath house is going up this summer, in the border of the city where they intend conveying the water by pipes, and to have prepared both founts and shower baths. The temperature at the boiling springs is 130 deg. *fahrenheit*. As this is rather too hot for bathing purposes, but little use has heretofore been made of these hot springs. The whole mountain side and part of the valley adjacent, exhibits evident indications of volcanic action, at some former period. And the high temperature of the springs, indicates the belief, that they must now have some connection with the phenomena of nature, involving the eternal fires of the earth.

JULY 26. — Travelled fifteen miles; encamped early on a small creek, running from the mountain to the lake. A very old Indian whom we had seen by the road at the crossing, came into camp towards night. A small piece of buffalo skin was his entire dress, with a pair of old moccasins. We gave the old man some victuals with which he seemed well pleased; eating part of his provision, greedily, and carefully wrapping the rest in a corner of his buffalo skin. He appeared very talkative and anxious to converse, but we could only gather a scattering idea of his discourse, and that more from his gestures than his words. How he had become detached from his tribe or band, and left in such a helpless condition, we could not ascertain.

JULY 27. — Travelled twelve miles to Capt. Brown's settlement, the last in the valley. The day was very warm, and though we made but a small march, yet the road being over a dry sandy plain, and near the base of the mountain, where we received the reflection of the heat in addition to its direct rays, we were quite exhausted on reaching camp about 10 o'clock, where we had a favorable place for our teams and also for ourselves.

JULY 28.—Exchanged most of our cattle for fresh ones, giving two yoke for one, or a handsome boot in a direct exchange; drove fifteen miles and encamped by an excellent spring at the base of the mountain, along the stream of which was excellent grass.

JULY 29.—Sabbath, remained in camp enjoying the luxury of a pure cold fountain of water just at hand, which at this season and in this hot and sandy valley, affords the greatest luxury on the route. We found nothing wanting to the sabbath's rest, but the privileges of the sanctuary, for which we substituted the reading of the bible, and other appropriate books, and exercises of private devotion.

JULY 30.—I started after breakfast, in company with another to ascend a mountain, at the base of which we were encamped; but after walking two or three hours, returned, the day growing warm, and finding the ascent slow and difficult, we thought the point we had reached was half way to the summit, but on viewing it from the valley, was disappointed, and somewhat amused to find that we had not been one fourth of the way up. In our short march to-day, crossed several streams of excellent water, cold and pure, heading in the mountain gorges, and running into the lake. Encamped in the evening on a small stream of good water.

JULY 31.—We travelled nineteen miles, crossing Bear river, and Muddy creek. We were obliged to ferry the river, being several rods wide and five or six feet deep. And here we had an example of extortion, man's inhumanity to man, even in taking advantage of his necessity in a pecuniary way. We were compelled from the necessity of the case, to pay a most exorbitant price for a ferriage privilege over this narrow stream. Encamped at a spring high on the mountain bluff to the right of the road.

AUG 1.—We had some difficulty in finding our cattle in the morning, and having understood that the Indians were troublesome in the vicinity, were apprehensive that they had driven them off in the night. But we found them all in an hour or two, and were soon on march. We passed a hot spring in two miles, and reached the large hot spring about 1 o'clock, 16 miles from our last encampment. The day being excessively warm and the road very dusty, we were exhausted and thirsty on reaching these springs, and seeing the springs pouring out their clear and apparently pure waters, hastened to drink of the same, when we found the water both warm and brackish. We found some however, of a temperature sufficiently cool to drink in small quantities, and at the same time a sufficient quantity of water for our cattle. Now we must either camp here for the night, or go twelve miles farther; and after resting awhile we decided on the latter;

resuming our dry and dusty march. Having reached water about 9 o'clock at night, a tolerable spring up a ravine to the right of the road, we found a number encamped here, and were obliged to stop nearly a mile from the spring to secure anything of a good camp ground. We prepared a hasty supper and were soon enjoying that luxury which is always sweetened by toil, "sleep, tired nature's restorer, balmy sleep."

AUG 2. — Travelled twelve miles, crossing a deep creek; a handsome and rapid little stream, and encamped early by a smaller stream affording good water and plenty of pasture along its banks. The wild sage again becomes very plenty here, and furnishes abundance of fuel. This artemesia or wild sage, with all vegetation except along the water courses, has become dried up for the want of rain, and great care is necessary to prevent campfires from breaking out and running over the whole country. Extensive districts are burnt over, along the road already; and it is feared by some that the little pasture remaining from the drouth, may be so destroyed with the burning of the grass, that it will be difficult to find forage enough for the teams on the road, involving the entire route yet to be traversed.

AUG 5. — Travelled twenty miles across a level plain or valley, covered almost throughout its whole extent with wild sage. We passed a tolerable spring at noon, which was all the water we had during the day. In the evening we encamped by a good spring on the mountain side, to the left of the road, from which we had a good view of the valley through which we had passed, and which extended on southward to the lake.

AUG 4. — Drove 20 miles to a creek in our pathway, where we remained until the 6th, the 5th being the Sabbath day. We had good grass and water and every accommodation of a good camp, which was fortunate for us after a hard week's travel, under a hot sun, over parched sandy plains, variegated only with occasional stony bluffs, hills and spars and mountains.

AUG 5. — Proceeded nine miles up this creek, thence six miles to the junction of the roads coming to Fort Hall and the lake. — Encamped three miles further on, by a good spring, but found the pasture near watering places entirely eaten up. Drove our cattle up a ravine coming out of the mountain, where we found tolerable grass for the night.

AUG 7. — We proceeded on our laborious journey, striking Goose creek about noon, having travelled 18 miles. The road to this creek was extremely rough, but it became good again on the bottom of the creek, where we found good company nearly all along.

AUG 8. — We proceeded up Goose creek eighteen miles to where the road leaves it. Encamped by an excellent spring, but no grass could be obtained for cattle without driving them a mile or more from camp.

AUG 9. — We left camp by daylight and drove eight or ten miles, over a sandy barren and rough piece of country where we stopped an hour to rest, and turned our cattle out to graze, more through formality than any prospect of finding grass. Arrived in Hot Spring valley in the afternoon, where we encamped by a large spring of cold water, having made a journey of 17 miles for the day. We drove our cattle a couple of miles to grass, where we left them for the night. Two of the men remained to guard them, as reports were out that the Indians had stolen a considerable number.

AUG 10. — Proceeded up the valley 14 miles, where finding good grass and water, we encamped for the night. The next morning being August the 11th, we made as early a start as possible, and travelled 18 miles, to the head of the valley where we found no grass, but excellent water. As we had no prospect of pasture for several miles on the road; we encamped by the spring, and drove our cattle out a mile to a ravine running through the mountains; where we found tolerable feed, but drove them in again before returning to our tents for the repose of the night, rather than run the risk of their being stolen by the Indians, as numbers of these savages were in the valley, and current reports that they had lately stolen a number of mules and cattle.

AUG 12. — Remained in camp according to our usual custom, this day being the holy Sabbath unto the Lord.

AUG 13. — We were on the road early in the morning, and ascended a long hill, from which we descended by a narrow ravine, reaching out into an extensive plain, on which the road forked, a branch running each side. We took the left, it being apparently the oldest track. Travelled to our usual camping time, without finding any water except a pond from which we watered our cattle, at noon. We were apprehensive for a time, that we would find no water for the night, but proceeding down the valley for a few miles, found several springs of excellent water, of remarkable depth, being six or eight feet deep. Here we encamped for the night, having travelled twenty miles.

AUG 14. — Proceeded down the river to Humboldt river, twenty miles. We enjoyed the advantage of a good road all day. The valley is level, about three or four miles wide, and affords excellent grass and water.

AUG 15th, 16th and 17th. — We proceeded down the river about eighteen miles per day, having a good road except the dust, and plenty of grass and water. A hurricane of wind that darkened the air with dust, passed over us on the 17th, continuing perhaps half an hour, with all the apparent fury characterizing the simoon of the desert.

AUG 18. — Reached Martins fork of the river about noon, where we remained over Sabbath. Drove a mile up the fork. Found an abundance of pasture and two springs, so large that they constituted the fork itself, a smart creek of pure cold water. The river where the road first strikes is no larger than an ordinary creek; but increases in size rapidly from its tributaries. It runs along a beautiful valley of irregular width and rich soil, walled on each side by barren, but beautiful mountain bluffs, without any timber but a few scattering cedar shrubs, and scarcely any vegetation whatever. The Shosonies [*sic*] or Snake Indians, inhabit the surrounding country, the region about this part of the river. A number came to our camp yesterday while eating dinner. They appeared well disposed to emigrants, and of correct deportment generally. But they were destitute even of arms, and fine specimens of nature's noblemen, "model artists of the wilderness," almost in an entire state of nudity, bidding defiance to those peculiarities of civilization, by which the essential beauties or deformities of the person are concealed from the public eye.

AUG 20. — Having rested the previous day — the day of rest divinely appointed, we started early and drove 20 miles through a rough, barren Kenyon to the river again, where finding the grass very scarce, we were compelled to drive three miles further, before camping, making in all 23 miles. The day was warm and sultry, the road rough and from 6 to 12 inches deep with dry dust, that both rendered it difficult and unpleasant for man or animal to travel or rather to trail over in its whole extent.

We found but a scant supply of water from a small spring or two in the Kenyon, and both men and teams were quite overcome with the most exhausting fatigue, on reaching the place of our encampment, where we had the river for our supply of water, and tolerable pasture for our cattle.

AUG 21. — We advanced down the river twelve miles, where finding pasture, and learning that it was poor for some distance ahead, we encamped for the night, spending a few leisure hours as best suited our dispositions and convenience in fishing, bathing &c.

AUG 22. — Travelled fifteen miles and encamped early, expecting James Watt, with his family (formerly of Jefferson county, O.) up in the evening. They arrived before sun down, and we, *viz*: McConnell and myself, travelled in company with them. Scott, Hoge, Haines and Maxfield with whom we had been in company, having moved on a few miles in advance of us the same evening.

AUG 23. — We left camp at 6 o'clock, and soon diverged from the river over a dry sandy plain of 12 miles, to where we again touched the river. Here we found no grass. The road was very dusty and the day warm. We turned our cattle among the willows along the river to rest rather than feed, before dinner. We dined down in the channel of the river by the water's edge, as the coolest and most secluded place from the dust that we could possibly find. A heavy gale of wind passed over just as we were leaving, that darkened the air with dust, and rendered it impossible to proceed for a short time. It remained cloudy during the afternoon, and fell a smart drizzling shower after night, slightly laying the dust for the following day. It was a late hour at night when we encamped; having travelled twenty-five miles, and previous to this late hour, having found no good grass; no adequate pasture for our poor animals.

AUG 24. — Travelled 15 miles, leaving the river, the most of the afternoon, over a sandy barren plain, we touched it again about 4 o'clock, when finding tolerable pasture, we encamped.

AUG 25. — Advanced on our journey 18 miles, leaving the river in the afternoon, passing over a heavy, sandy road for five or six miles. The sun was intensely hot, and a number of the oxen, belonging to James Watt, and two teams in company gave out, and were left until the next morning. Our own team was much fatigued on reaching camp on the river, where we obtained good grazing and laid up as usual, on the Sabbath, the 26th of this hot month.

AUG 27. — Proceeded down the river 18 miles. Here the river bottom for several miles, becomes low and marshy. It was covered with tall grass and reeds, affording a good range of cattle. But the water having no regular running current, was of the most inferior kind. Encamped by the edge of the marsh, where a well two or three feet deep, dug by preceeding emigrants, afforded us tolerable water.

AUG 28. — We advanced along our journey about 15 miles, when finding good pasture we encamped, and on the morning of the 29th, we left camp early, crossed the river four times during the day. Travelled twenty miles and had grazing of the best quality. The teams of Mr. Watt with whom myself and McConnel had been associated for some time, now seemed entirely exhausted, and he determined to lay up for some days and recruit them. It became necessary for us, however, to move on, and we reluctantly left Mr. Watt and his family this morning.

AUG 30. — We had heard some days back of a new road, leaving the old one, 70 or 80 miles above the sink of the river, bearing North of West to Feather river, and finding numbers recruiting here and cutting grass for a desert of sixty miles on the first of the road; we also cut some with a view of taking this new route, in accordance with the representation that it was the nearest and best route. Drove five miles and grazed our oxen the remainder of the day.

AUG 31. — We passed on fourteen miles to where the new road leaves the one, a point at which we stopped to graze, but found poor pasture, as it had all been eaten off by teams laying up before taking the stretch on the new road. We here learned that there was some uncertainty about the new road being opened across the Sierra Nevada mountains, and hence determined to take the old route. After driving six miles further, making twenty miles in all during the day, although we found no pasture we were obliged to encamp for the night.

SEPT 1st. — Travelled twenty miles. We encountered a sand bluff in a few miles, which proved very laborious, tedious and positively perplexing in our efforts to pass through. We touched the river near Sun down, but found no pasture except weeds and willows. The bluffs came in very close proximity to the river here, leaving but a narrow bottom, and consequently but little grass; and the advanced teams at this time had entirely eaten it up for miles around camping points.

SEPT 2nd. — It is once more the Sabbath. McConnell and myself are alone in the wilderness. We have laid up here in our usual observance of the Lord's day. It is a dreary barren spot, but the Lord Jehovah is here. The universe is his great Temple, — and the devout worshipper can every where look up to his Father in Heaven and be in fellowship with him. We spent that day and night without any thing to molest us, but the wolves appeared to have an instinctive knowledge of our situation. They kept up a tremendous howling around us, and occasionally came up to our wagon. They even approached to our very camp tables, devouring the crumbs and bones that had fallen from it. We rose once in the night and took out our rifles to give them a salute, but they disappeared and kept their distance till we again retired. The rascals had, no doubt, smelled powder before now; and, concluding that prudence was the better part of valor, they deprived us of an opportunity of stretching their uncircumcised carcasses upon the sandy plain.

SEPT 3rd. — We departed from our encampment at an early hour. Ascended a bluff again — proceeded over a heavy sandy road, and touched the river at noon without finding pasture. — Having travelled fifteen miles, we encamped on the border of the bluff, turning our cattle on the narrow bottom of the bluff below, where, indeed, there was no grazing but some green willows that afforded a very meager substitute for the same.

SEPT 4th. — We continued on the bluff fifteen miles, crossing four miles before reaching the river, where we found some grass. We encamped, at the close of this day's journey, by a well on the border of the large slough that here commences and continues to the sink of the river. D. Brewer, bearer of government dispatches to Fort Hall, staid [sic] with us to-night.

SEPT 5th. — We moved ten miles down the river, where, still finding good grass, we encamped to recruit our oxen, as much as time would permit, before entering on the desert just before us. Here we cut off part of our wagon-bed to lighten our load, and mowed sufficient grass to carry with us for two days' rations, as there is none for 60 or 70 miles after leaving that point.

SEPT 6th. — We drove to the sink of the river, where we found a few wells of strong sulphur water—the best, in fact, which the point afforded. We had understood that a mountain stream afforded water at this place; but we were disappointed. No such happy providential arrangement was to be found. We watered our teams at the wells, and used freely of it ourselves, overcome as we were with the most demanding thirst. To all it was very unpalatable and to some sickening. It soon made visible demonstrations on my corporeal system. From this point we had 50 miles to travel across a barren sandy waste, properly called, by emigrants, the "Waste" or "Desert"—being, in fact, the Northern point of the "Great Western Desert," marked on our Geographical Charts. Having been disappointed in procuring water at the sink of the river, we found ourselves now 20 miles past a watering point, and 50 miles before reaching any but a few wells of salty, brackish water along the road over the desert—wells that have been dug by emigrants in hopes of good water, but in vain. The water which they afforded can scarcely be used at all, proving rather an aggravation than a gratification of thirst. We left this place at 10 o'clock at night, just as the welcome moon appeared in the horizon; and travelled 20 miles by daylight, when we stopped an hour at one of these wells, the water of which even our cattle refused. Here we took some breakfast and fed on the hay which we carried with us. Having proceeded 10 miles further, and finding the day growing very warm, we lay up till 2 o'clock P.M. We had left the sink in company with a small train from Missouri—the Rough and Ready train—which proved a fortunate circumstance at this time for us; otherwise we might have been under the necessity of waiting for another train. Our team was reduced to two yoke of oxen, and they much fatigued and worn by a long journey, and poor pasture for most of the last 100 miles. One of our cattle gave out before reaching the sink, on the day previous, and we thought ourselves fortunate in getting another in his place, for which we paid a fair price; but the new ox gave out that night, and we left both on the road, having only one yoke to our wagon. The road became very heavy with sand; and, considering it impossible to proceed with one yoke, we made an arrangement with Mr. Brown, of the train, to carry our baggage through for our remaining team, giving, as we thought, the best we could under the circumstances. In the afternoon, the train was again on the road. And McConnell and I having no charge now in the way of teams or wagon, took our rifles and went on in advance, little thinking we had twenty miles of deep and sandy road to travel over before reaching water. We had come 40 or 50 miles without any but a little sulphur water obtained at the sink of the river, which, instead of benefiting me, had so sickened me that I could not eat, and, consequently, was in bad condition for wading 20 miles under a scorching Sun through sand from 6 to 12 inches deep. — We had proceeded but a short distance till we realized our situation, and, perhaps, would have taken advantage from the shade of some wagon left along the road, of which we observed many as we passed along—and here have remained till Sun down; but, deceived in the distance, we proceeded as fast as we could, expecting soon to reach water, the want of which I had never felt to the same extent before. Near Sun down we reached a well of salt water, from which we received great benefit by bathing in it, but could not drink it, for it a few sups were forced it only aggravated our raging thirst. Carson river was before us. The thought of its refreshing and pure waters still kept up hope and life; but we had ten miles of a journey yet to accomplish, and it seemed double that distance under our circumstances of distress. Every minute seemed an hour—every mile a league; but the tenacity of life is wonderful, and the love of it is natural to man. To sink down on the sandy plain and die the horrible death from thirst, was a catastrophe most dreadful in the contemplation; and our very thirst imparts new energy to every element of life. The vital organs seem to be fortified in proportion to the difficulties of our position, and the very dangers to which we have adverted. At last, about the hour of midnight, or, perhaps, a little after, we reached Carson river. Our first impulse was to plunge ourselves into the stream, and we were only restrained from such a reckless transaction by the consideration that we had no change of clothes at hand. We contented ourselves by drinking copiously and bathing. The idea of supper scarcely entered our heads. — We had taken no supper, in fact we had none to take. — The sensation of hunger was lost in one of greater magnitude. Our thirst was quenched, hunger was forgotten, — a camp fire kindled on the river bank — a blanket providentially obtained—and we made a rapid excursion to the land of somnus and of pleasant dreams. — And lifting up our eyes and hearts to a kind Heavenly Father, we could, in a moment, spiritualize the events of the day. How refreshing the waters of spiritual life to the thirsty soul. How welcome the rest of Heaven on the banks of the river of life,—after our journey through this earthly desert—this dreary wilderness where no water of Heaven's perfect blessedness is to be found by the poor pilgrim with his face set towards the "city of gold" on high. The teams did not arrive till near morning—jaded and almost entirely worn out. Every team had left a part of its oxen by the way. Some of these animals were afterwards brought in; but others never revived. The whole road was strewed with dead cattle, mules and horses, wagon carts, chairs, telling each succeeding emigrant, what he too well learned before getting over, that it was a desperate point in the route.

The first week in September has now almost passed away. The Sabbath is once more with us. And thankful to God for his goodness, we remain here till the beginning of the second week of September, when we resumed our toilsome pilgrimage. How beautiful does this river appear in our eyes now! It seems the sweetest river we have ever seen! What delightful and exhilerating waters! We trace the river to its source. It is up in yonder mountains. The stream comes rolling down cool and clear and abundant—the bountiful provision of God for a mighty population in the future—and now the very temporal salvation of us weary emigrants to the shores and valleys and hills lined with that, the "love of which is the root of all evil."

Having disposed of our teams and baggage, we had no charge whatever, and wishing to reach the point of destination for which we had long and arduously labored, we now set out on foot, without provisions or bedding with the hope of securing them from advanced emigrants. For the most part, our expectations were realized. But successful as we were, it was rather nominal than real. Our sleeping accommodations are not worthy to be celebrated on the pages of history or in the song of the poet. At the best, they were miserably poor, and once or twice no place whatever, but mother earth. Still we thought of the Patriarch Jacob, and were content. From dry pine we made a large fire, and the spirit of Yankee invention was stirred within us, when we attempted to make a bed out of pine bushes. But our success was not very complimentary to our inventive powers, as we could not succeed in adjusting these bushes so as to be entirely comfortable.

One week brought us to Pleasant Valley, or the dry diggins, a distance of over two hundred miles from the point where we struck Carson river. We followed up this river one hundred miles before we struck the mountains, for the place of our destination.

CHAPTER SIX

Journey from Pleasant Valley to San Francisco

t last we have emerged from our long and perilous journey into the borders of that land, which like many other earthly things, will never fulfill the promises with which these objects of the imagination have been invested. The insignia of busy and civilized life are now around us. The sight if a log cabin is a real luxury, and to sit down to a table and eat a regular meal with fresh beef and vegetables, proved almost too much of a temptation for our desperate appetites. After taking a general view of the operations in this mining district, we procured some tools, a pick, shovel and pan, and went to work digging gold. But how experience often changes the glowing visions, into cold realities. We had been informed on the whole way, that an ordinary day's labor would always insure an ounce or more of the precious metal. But we labored all day and got nothing, and ascertained further, that this was the lot of many others. The second day proved no better, and the third no better in the way of success. My partner, McConnel being a carpenter, now concluded to go on to Sacramento City, and engage in that business, which he did in a few days. I remained eight or nine days still working in the mines, or gold placers; and fortunately during the few days, took out several ounces per day. Our baggage having been directed to Sacramento City, and having heard nothing of McConnel, as I expected, I resolved to proceed on down, procure my baggage and make some permanent arrangement for winter. I reached the city about the 1st of October, where I had a severe attack of dysentery, by which I was very much prostrated for some time. While I was in a state of convalescence, I met with McElrath and Rainy, of our original company, and others who had come to the city for provisions, intending to winter in southern California. McConnel and myself engaged to go with them, and purchased a yoke of cattle and put in with their team. Our arrangements made, we were again on the road with fine weather, and good prospects, as usual, going to the mines. We landed on Curtis creek between Stanislaus and Tuolumne rivers, after ten days travel, a distance of 150 miles. Here we landed and pitched our tents, calculating soon to build a cabin for winter. Not finding the place to yield,

47

in accordance with our anticipations and with the prospect of a hard winter before us, and high provisions in the mining district, Rainy, McConnel and myself concluded to go on to the coast for the winter. The roads had become bad from the recent heavy rains, and though we came back to the river in an empty mule wagon, we were three days on the road. We reached Stockton in the early part of November, and found the whole town almost blockaded with mud. It is situated on a slough running up several miles from a river in the vicinity of the place. We secured lodging at what was called the Branch hotel. It was a long one-story building, divided into two rooms. The first of these answered for a bar room and parlor, the second, for dining and sleeping room; a small lobby at one end of the building was the kitchen. We succeeded in getting a place to stand in the first mentioned apartment, till the supper bell rang, when those next the door had the fortune to get a seat at the first table, and the others their room. Supper over, we spread our beds in the dining room, and fared better in sleeping than for some time. On the 12th of November, Rainy and myself set out for San Francisco, on board a small schooner. Had bad weather and an unpleasant trip — landing on the 15th, at the great commercial emporium of California. McConnel went by the way of Sacramento City from Stockton, to get our trunks, which had been stored there; and he did not arrive for some days afterwards. We found the city almost impassible along the streets next the river. It still continued to rain, and every thing combined to give the place a gloomy, rather than a pleasant and attractive appearance. We stopped for a few days at a Restaurant boarding house on Clay St., when we removed to the Revere hotel at the north point of the city.

Rainy and McConnel went into the trading business; and I having received an appointment as Inspector of the port of San Francisco, from Col. Collier; went on board a Dutch brig, *North Pole*, on the 25th of November, where I remained till the 1st of January, 1850.

My debut as Inspector was rather discouraging. The cabin was small and hampered, and the captain a selfish and most unaccommodating son of Neptune. I slept about a week on a small sofa in the cabin, and had to complain to the authorities of the Custom House, before I could procure a berth. And even then, my bed was sail cloth, and my bed clothes a blanket and cloak. — On the 9th of Januray, I went aboard the barque *Conception*, as Inspector. The vessel although from Chili, was commanded by Americans. Captain Howis, I found quite a gentleman, and enjoyed myself well on his vessel.

Here the regular journal is arrested in its course; having come apparently to an abrupt termination. Still the design originally contemplated, has been fully accomplished. A condensed memorandum has been given, respecting the writer's journey from Steubenville to the Metropolitan city, on the shores of the Pacific Ocean. And from detached papers and letters, we gather his remaining history up to the period of his death. A short time subsequent to the last record made in his journal, he took an excursion to the mines on the Yuba river, and there engaged in the enterprise of a provision store. But he soon returned to San Francisco with his health much impaired. In the month of August, 1850, having embarked on a vessel for New York city, and having arrived in safety, our young friend was bouyant with hope that he would soon be in the bosom of his friends and relatives, in the state of Ohio. He had proceeded on his way as far as the city of Buffalo, and there breathed his last among strangers, but a few hours before an affectionate brother arrived to meet him, and with a hearty welcome, convey him to "his own home."

Soon after his death, the following obituary notice appeared in one of our leading periodicals:—

"Died, on Sabbath morning, the 6th of October, 1850, of typhoid fever, in the city of Buffalo, on his way home from California, Mr. SAMUEL RUTHERFORD DUNDASS, in the 31st year of his age.

The deceased was a brother of the Rev. John R. Dundass, pastor of Mingo Church, Pa. While a student of Princeton Theological Seminary, his letters to this younger brother, now in his grave, it is believed, were mainly instrumental in his conversion to God, and his subsequent resolution to seek the requisite preparation himself for the gospel ministry. He accordingly commenced, and for some time prosecuted a course of study, with a view to this great purpose of his life. But a constitutional disease developed itself in the form of chronic bronchitis, attended with physical debility, which compelled him to abandon his original design and engage in some pursuit where public speaking would not be brought into requisition. He then read the usual course of medicine, but with the prevailing impression that he never would be able to enter actively upon the duties of that laborious profession.

After having for a time filled an important civil office in Jefferson county, Ohio—the place of his nativity—and finding the door providentially closed against his continuance in that public position, unfettered by business or domestic ties, he resolved to test the supposed genial influence of some foreign clime. Despair of help from the common remedies, and having read some accounts of remarkable cures effected by a journey through the Plains and over the Rocky Mountains, he was induced to try the experiment, as a kind of forlorn hope, for his health—making pecuniary considerations, as he declared to his friends, altogether subordinate in the case. And contrary to the expectations of those who felt the deepest interest in his welfare, he was preserved through the perilous journey of the wilderness, and his consumptive malady apparently removed—having better health last winter in San Francisco than he had previously enjoyed for many years. But during the past summer the symptoms of his former disease returned with such violence as to threaten a fatal termination; and having embarked for home in the month of August, he arrived in New York city about the 24th of September, and was trying to reach the residence of a near and dear relative in Medina County, Ohio—most anxiously wishing, no doubt, to die in the arms of his friends. The mournful privilege, however, neither he nor his friends were permitted to enjoy. In Buffalo city he was prostrated with a violent attack of the prevailing fever; and before his brother arrived, whom he had summoned by a telegraphic dispatch to his dying bed, he had breathed his last. His remains were taken immediately to the residence of his brother, in Ohio, and deposited in the graveyard where he himself expects to repose, when the toils of life and the agonies of death shall have passed away.

The subject of this notice has left a journal and many interesting letters written in his absence, that may yet be given to the public, for the gratification of numerous friends who manifested their friendship towards him in various ways during his life, and who have already expressed their sympathy with the surviving relatives in this sad bereavement. In one of his letters written previous to his departure from Steubenville for the shores of the Pacific, in reply to objections urged by his brother to his contemplated journey, expressing the fear that he would in all probability die among strangers, without the soothing and consolatory attention of friends around him in his last moments, he uses the following language: "To live with friends and acquaintances of early life, and have them stand by our side in sickness and death, may be desired by all, but comparatively few enjoy the boon. Joseph slept in a land of strangers, and Moses in a lone desert mountain, and many have succeeded them both. If we are prepared for an exchange of worlds, it is not very material to us where that exchange takes place—at home or abroad—in the arms of strangers or of friends." Passing, however, the grave of an emigrant in his route, he records this reflection in his journal at the time: "Society is so dear to man, that even to see the grave of a departed one, in the wide uninhabited plain or desert, suggests solitary emotions, and instinctively excites that feeling so common to us all—a desire to sleep with our fathers." His last letters, especially, show that he was living near to Jesus, and that his affections were placed, not on the treasures of the golden land, but on the golden streets of the heavenly city. "It is my sincere desire," he writes, "my fixed resolution, to live to the glory of God, that by his grace I may be prepared for a longer life, or fitted for an earlier death." I desire to take a very low place at the feet of Jesus Christ; and I cherish a hope which, as an anchor to my soul, I would not exchange for worlds." A few days before his death, he sketched with a pencil, in a tremulous and scarcely legible hand, his last communication to one of his brothers, concluding with two sentences expressive of the state of his mind in view of approaching dissolution: "I trust in the immutable promises of God, and pray

50

for their fulfillment in my case. If I should never see my friends again, while life remains, I will still pray for them."

Many considerations tend to render this a most afflictive dispensation of Divine Providence. The deceased was the youngest member of an affectionate family. He was amiable, honorable and upright—endowed with an intellect of a superior order, and abounding in that noble generosity which disposed him to sacrifice his own comfort with a view to contribute to the happiness of others. Had he died on the plains, or in the midst of the mountains, or in the valley of the Sacramento; he might at least have had acquaintances around him, and his death under such circumstances would have been nothing more than his friends expected. But after having heard of his remarkable preservation, and apparent restoration to health, while thousands stronger than he had fallen victims to disease and death; and while his brothers and sisters, having received intelligence that he was on his way home, were waiting every day with the most anxious solitude to see him—to hear in the meantime of his death so near his friends, and yet among strangers, renders the bereavement inexpressibly sad. How mysterious is the course of Divine Providence! How hard under such circumstances is it sometimes, even for the pious friends to say, "The will of the Lord be done." And whatever may be their resignation in view of the loss they have sustained, they feel justified by eminent examples in sacred history, when they mourn and "go to the grave to weep there."

But while the bleeding hearts of surviving relatives almost refuse to be comforted, calm reflection, under the influence of Christian feelings, teaches that God does all things well. And submission to his holy providence is here urged, both by dictates of reason and the leading elements in the religion of Christ. However dark the cloud may be, there is to the believer a sun behind that cloud. It is the prerogative of Jehovah to be his own interpreter in all the mysteries of his providential government. What we know not now we shall know hereafter, is the blessed assurance that he has given us from his infallible word. And in the gloomiest shade of this affliction, there are still even now some rays of light. If early piety, if a consistent deportment; if elevated religious experience, be an index to a happy immortality, then death, in the case of this beloved young man, is everlasting gain. He remembered his Creator in the days of his early youth, connecting himself with the people of God, as a member of the Presbyterian Church, in the 19th year of his age. He had not yet arrived at the meridian of life, but at the same time he had been called to experience, in their various forms some of the sorrows common to humanity, and some peculiar to his providential lot in life. Some years ago the domestic circle to which he belonged, was broken up by the removal of two of its leading members to the silent tomb—a widowed mother and a beloved sister leaving him, as he often expressed himself, without a home in this world, and producing a shock to the tender sensibilities of his nature from which he never fully recovered. — And in his last illness, doubtless, when he saw around him no sister, or brother, or friend, or acquaintance, to administer to his wants, or speak words of comfort to him in a dying hour, he was led to think of bygone days, when in sickness he had a mother's love and a sister's affectionate care. Now when the promptings of his heart would wish for their presence around his sick bed, we have reason to believe that his desires were more than realized by the interposition of a heavenly Father, sending kind angels to visit his sick and dying chamber, to bear away his emancipated spirit to the home and rest of God's people, there to be forever associated with those dear departed friends whose lives constituted the elements of his happy home on earth.

THE JOURNALS OF
SAMUEL RUTHERFORD DUNDASS
&
GEORGE KELLER
CROSSING THE PLAINS
TO CALIFORNIA IN 1849-1850

THE JOURNAL OF GEORGE KELLER CROSSING THE PLAINS TO CALIFORNIA IN 1850

YE GALLEON PRESS
FAIRFIELD, WASHINGTON

A TRIP ACROSS THE PLAINS,

AND

LIFE IN CALIFORNIA;

EMBRACING

A DESCRIPTION OF THE

OVERLAND ROUTE;

Its Natural Curiosities,

RIVERS, LAKES, SPRINGS, MOUNTAINS, INDIAN

TRIBES, &c. &c. ;

THE GOLD MINES

OF CALIFORNIA:

Its Climate, Soil, Productions,

Animals, &c.,

WITH SKETCHES

Of Indian, Mexican and Californian

Character :

To which is Added,

A GUIDE OF THE ROUTE

FROM THE MISSOURI RIVER TO THE PACIFIC OCEAN.

BY GEO. KELLER,
PHYSICIAN TO THE WAYNE COUNTY COMPANY.

TABLE OF CONTENTS

NAMES AND RESIDENCE

OF EACH MEMBER OF THE

WAYNE COUNTY COMPANY

(TAKEN ON BOARD THE STEAMBOAT, *CONSIGNEE*.)

Luther M. Dennison,	Wooster, Ohio.	†A. Thornton, Milton,	W'yne co.
*Daniel C. Loyd,	do.	†James Jackson,	do. do.
Frederick Kouk,	do.	*David Peffer,	Wooster, Ohio.
William Duck,	Dalton, O.	*John Mahaffie,	do. do.
Henry Duch,	do.	John France,	do. do.
John Murrow,	do.	George Fleck,	do. do.
Cyrus Youcum,	Plain t'p. Wa'ne co. Ohio.	Jesse Weirick,	Dalton, Wayne co O.
Benj. Eason,	do.	Alex, Clark,	do. do.
David Soliday,	do.	Samuel Thomas,	do. do.
Henry Soliday,	do.	Franklin Thomas,	do. do.
*Alexander Eason,	do.	*John Bell,	do. do.
Joshua Eberhart,	do.	Chas. N. Lamison,	do. do.
Eli Jones,	do.	Isaac Bailey,	do. do.
Wm. Allenbaugh,	do.	James Elder,	do. do.
John Kimmell, Canaan,	do.	Henry Wertz,	do. do.
Lewis Barritt,	do. do.	Franklin Myer,	do. do.
Baltzer Houck,	do. do.	Mark Elder,	do. do.
Henry Mowry, E. Union,	do.	‡Joseph Sturgiss,	do. do.
Nathaniel Ames,	do. do.	Jacob Updegraff,	do. do.
John Keffer, Wooster,	do. do.	Israel Homan,	do. do.
David Bower, Chester,	do. do.	Martin Hoover,	do. do.
G.R. M'Intire, Franklin,	do. do.	Daniel Hoover,	do. do.
B. Mutersbaugh, Plain,	do. do.	Thomas Marshall,	do. do.
H. Drabenstadt, Green,	do. do.	Edward Briggs,	do. do.
Sam'l. Hanson, Wooster,	do. do.	Levi Scott,	do. do.
Henry Ammerman,	do. do.	John Keller,	do. do.
Jared Campbell,	do. do.	Joseph Harper,	do. do.
Joseph Jackson,	do. do.	Elijah M'Dowell,	do. do.
*Lewis Gibson,	do. do.	John Cully,	do. do.
Wesley P. Yordy,	do. do.	Peter Cully,	do. do.
J. Mendenhall,	Lakeport, Ia.	Henry Oberlin,	Dalton, Wayne co. O.
†John Huffstodt,	Wooster, O.	Samuel M'Clelland,	do. do.
†Thos. Smith,	do. do.	W.F.E. Clark,	do. do.
†Charles Miller,	do. do.	Boyd Clark,	do. do.
†Matthew M'Clure,	do. do.	Wm. H. Smith,	do. do.
†Jonathan M'Clure,	do. do.	David Gearhart,	do. do.

GEORGE KELLER

Dr. Geo. Keller,	do.	do.	John Robinson,	do.	do.
Benj. Wilcox,	do.	do.	Martin Mathis,	do.	do.
Jas. M. Vaughn,	Wooster, t'p, O.		Joseph Karnes,	do.	do.
John Pearson,	Dalton, W'ne co.		Abram Smith,	do.	do.
*Thos. M'Clelland,	Sugar cr. t. W'ne co. O.		Philip Swartz,	do.	do.
Thos. Latimer,	do.		Edwin H. Miles,	Guilford, Medina co. O.	
†Christian Fuek,	do.	do.	John Coble,	Lake tp. Ashland co. O.	
Andrew Murray,	Dalton, Ohio		Elijah Runyan,	do.	do.
R.R. Gailey,	do.	do.	Wm. Doolittle,	do.	do.
J. Gailey,	do.	do.	John Stover,	do.	do.
S. Coe, Baughman, tp.	W. co. O.		Simon Stewart,	do.	do.
Isaiah Bates, Dalton,	do.	do.	Mich'l Stewart,	do.	do.
Jos. Weirick,	Wooster, tp.		James Stewart,	Washington tp. Holmes co. O.	
†Dr. D. Weaver,	do.	vil'ge	J.W. Everstine,	Loudonville, O.	
†Quimby Jones,	do.	do.	Cornelius Dill,	do.	do.
Peter Garlock, Edingburgh	do.		Peter Lumbert,	do.	do.
Samuel Motter,	do.	do.	J. Miller,	do.	do.
James Brown,	do.	do.	Lemuel Miller,	do.	do.
Edwin E. Gorgas,	do.	do.	Jacob Likes,	do.	do.
John Elder,	do.	do.	Abram Likes,	do.	do.
John Reasor,	do.	do.	Jacob Emeric,	do.	do.
James Atkinson,	do.	do.	Thos. Peterson,	Morrow tp. Holmes co. O.	
R.K. Deverny,	do.	do.	Stutley Whitford,	Wayne co. O.	
†Jacob Stiver,	Wayne tp. do.		Sam'l. Charlton,	Ashland co. O.	
†Jacob Paulis,	do.	do.	John Springer,	do.	do.
†Nicholas Paulis,	do.	do.	Wm. Rice,	Medina co. O.	
†Benj. Lehman,	do.	do.	George Miller,	Ashland co. O.	
Geo. Sonedecker,	do.	do.	Philip Wolf,	Wayne co. do.	
A. Sonedecker,	do.	do.	†David Rhodes,	Stark co. do.	
Philip Proutman,	do.	do.	†John Miller,	do.	do.
William Yost,	do.	do.	†John Wagoner,	Summit co. do.	
Jacob Oswald,	do.	do.	†Jos. Callback,	do.	do.
Simon Ihrig,	do.	do.	†Peter Marsh,	do.	do.
George Wolf,	do.	do.	†John Alban,	Canal Fulton, O.	
Jesse Beighley,	Milton tp. do.		†A. Wolfbarger,	do.	do.
*David Kimberlin,	Green do. do.		†Franklin Babb,	Summit co. do.	
Mrs. D. Kimberlin,	do.	do.	*Wm. H. Paramor,	Mansfield do.	
John Long,	do.	do.	Geo. L. Jacobs,	do.	do.
Hugh M'Davitt,	do.	do.	Jacob Miller,	do.	do.
James Hoy, S'rcreek tp.	do.		Samuel Dillon,	do.	do.
Wm. M'Connell,	Massillon, O.		Daniel Dice,	do.	do.
Samuel Marsh,	do.	do.	Jas. M'Quade, jr.,	do.	do.
Gabriel Messersmith,	C'l Dover, O.		Thos. Paramor,	do.	do.
David Gochenour,	E. Union, do.		Thomas Barnd,	do.	do.
E.H. Webb,	Salem, O.		†D.L. Harris,	Summit co. O.	
S.R. Middleton,	do.	do.	†P.W. Reader,	Wayne co. do.	
David Karnes,	Canaan tp. W'yne co. O.		†Samuel Stover,	Sum'it co. do.	

†Adam Ruff, Fulton do.
†Jacob Weysogle, do. do.
†Thomas Thorpe, do. do.
Frank Lauderdale, Holmes co. do.
Geo. Lauderdale, do. do.
Thos. Gorsuch, Wayne co. do.
L. Whitside, do. do.
†Geo. Rudy, Greenville do.
†S. Rudy, do. do.
†Sam'l. Clendenney, do. do.
John Leish, Haysville, Ashland co. O.
A. Shroder, New Lisbon, O
Charles Nininger, do.
*Wm. M'Curdy, Canton do.
*L. Barral, do. do.
J. Dunbar, do. do.
Geo. Rhedben, do. do.
Jeremiah Gilford, do. do.
Geo. J. Bettinger, do. do.
Wm. Lessig, Dalton, W'e c. do.
D. Fletcher, do. do.
*M. Barclay, do. do.
J. Fletcher, do. do.
*S.D. Kauffman, Canton, O.
*E.M. Meffert, do. do.
*Henry Kauffman, do. do.
*George Stuck, do. do.
N.M.D. M'Millen, Mansfield, O.
John Dennison, do. do.
Wm. R. Hendricks, do. do.
S'l. Allenbaugh, Plain tp. W'ne co. O.
†J.P. Murphy, Freeport, Armstrong co. Pa.
†Geo. Brown, do. do.
†R.M. Porter, do. do.
†Robert Cooper, do. do.
†S.L. Combs, Kittaning, do.
†J. Bradley, Florence do.
†J.S. Lamb, Burgettstown do.
†R.B. Murser, Florence do.
†S. Hamlin, Harman's creek do.
†R. Biddle, Burgettstown do.
†R. Kennedy, do. do.
†A. Wilson, do. do.
†T.F. Fowle, Armstrong co. do.
†Jacob Milliron, do. do.
†Wm. Guthrie, do. do.
†S.B. Fowle, do. do.

†B. Rodgers, do. do.
†Thos. Farrow, Pittsburgh do.
†John Gumbert, do. do.
†Wm. Henry, do. do.
Henry Gumbert, do. do.
†Geo. Gumbert, do. do.
†B. Rook, do. do.
†Sam'l. Fleming, do. do.
†Wm. Smith, do. do.
†Robert Gregg, do. do.
†Robert Orton, do. do.
Hector Orton, do. do.
†Frank Robinson, do. do.
†Wm. Griffith, do. do.
†Josiah Boucher, Ligonier do.
†Isaac F. Boucher, do. do.
†David Boucher, do. do.
†John George, do. do.
Geo. Aurentz, Blairsville do.
Peter Uurentz, do. do.
Sam'l. C. Moorhead, do. do.
Joseph Aurentz, Pittsburg do.
†Mic'l. Lipe, Somerset co. do.
†Peter Lipe, do. do.
†S. Naugle, Laughlintown do.
†Jesse Griffith, Somerset co. do.
†David Griffith, do. do.
†Christian Stauff, do. do.
†Geo. Couster, Stoystown do.
†Jon. Smith, do. do.
Samuel Shire, Holmes co. O.
George Lee, do. do.
Reuben Spangler, do. do.
John Kinnard, Wooster do.
Slemon Lisle, Holmes co. O.
P.C. Chesrown, do. do.
J. Marvin, do. do.
M. Troyer, do. do.
Isaac Moon, do. do.
R. F. Cahill, Findlay do.
John M'Clelland, Dalton, Ohio joined the
company at St. Joseph.

* Dead.
† Went in another Company from St. Joseph
‡ Left sick at St. Laramie, from thence returned
to the States.

60

CHAPTER ONE

"Returned Californian"—"making a start for the Diggings."
Big Blue, Little Blue, and Platte Valley.

uring the early part of the year 1850, Mr. M. L. Dennison, a "returned Californian," visited our place, (Dalton, Wayne county, Ohio,) and gave such a glowing description of the "El Dorado," that considerable numbers from this and adjoining counties, began at once to make preparations, in order to reach the "Diggins" by the "Overland Route."

As Mr. Dennison was about returning to California, we concluded to place ourselves under his guidance, supposing of course, that he was well acquainted with the route, and necessary outfit. Getting together our wagons, harness, clothing, &c., we took passage on board the Steamer "Consignee," bound for St. Joseph, Mo., designing to leave the frontier at that point. We arrived at this place March 31st. Though raining violently, we at once began getting our wagons and buggies ashore, and selecting a camping place. We spent the ensuing week in buying stock, provisions, cooking utensils, and getting all things ready, before starting out, on a long, tedious journey. Horses were worth from fifty to one hundred dollars, and mules from seventy-five to one hundred and fifty.

The outfit among the messes, generally, was four mules or horses, and one wagon, to every four men. By the advice of our guide we took but fifty pounds of flour, and forty of hard bread, to each man; an amount we found wholly insufficient, as partial starvation, during the latter part of the route, satisfactorily demonstrated. Our other articles of provision were in about the same proportion.

On the 7th, 8th and 9th of April, the different messes crossed the Missouri river, and encamped near the bluff, six miles from St. Joseph's.

We found plenty of wood and good water at this point. A variety of the paroquet abounds in this part of the Indian territory. Mr. Mendenhall ascended a tree at this place, in pursuit of a squirrel, and, in endeavoring to capture it, inflicted a wound near his knee with a hatchet, which prevented him from travelling, "on foot," for a distance of one thousand miles.

On the evening of the 9th Mr. R. F. Cahill, of Findlay, Ohio, arrived at our camp, and engaged Messrs. Hoovers, of Dalton, to "take him through" to the "diggins."

Next morning, about 7 o'clock, we broke up our camp and after driving a few minutes, found ourselves on the almost boundless prairie. The scenery on these vast natural fields, creates, for a short time, an exhilirating effect on the mind of the traveller; but the sameness of the scene soon becomes monotonous.

This evening we encamped about two miles west of the "Indian Agency." As grass had not yet begun growing on the prairie, we were compelled to carry food for the mules and horses. Several of our messes bought corn at this place, paying one dollar per bushel.

We travelled this day about 27 miles. As many of the mules had never been harnessed before, of course some trouble might be expected in getting them to work well, — but I believe we had no "bawks," or runaways, during the day.

On Sunday afternoon (April 14th) we crossed the Big Blue, distant from St. Joseph about 125 miles. This stream is about 120 feet wide, and at this time about three feet deep. We forded it without any difficulty. Later in the season, during the heavy rains, this stream is swollen very much, and may detain a company several days, either in waiting for it "to fall," or in ferrying it. The weather, during the afternoon, was warm and pleasant; but the days preceding it, had been unusually cold, snowing frequently, with a cold wind from the north. In this distance we had no wood, except in the vicinity of streams. Next evening about sunset, we crossed Little Blue, and travelled near it the two successive days; the weather, during this time, cold and rainy.

Friday evening (19th) we struck the valley of Platte, or Nebraska river, and encamped near some pools of stagnant water, about three miles from the river. Not having any fuel here but prairie grass, and it wet by the rains, we concluded to dispense with the ceremony of getting supper, and therefore went to bed minus this meal.

CHAPTER TWO

*Fort Kearney—"Doby Houses,"—Buffalo, Deer, &c,—Ford of South
Platte—Encampment of Sioux—Fine Arts—Squaws.*

ext morning about sunrise, we started forward, intending to breakfast at Fort Kearney, distant about ten miles. Reaching this place about ten o'clock, we concluded to stop for an hour or two, during which time some breakfast was "got up," and flour was purchased to feed the stock, many of them being nearly worn out by hard driving, and an insufficient amount of food. Spring being unusually late, we, as yet, found no grass, and it became necessary to economize the grain we had with us as much as possible.

This military establishment is about 300 miles from St. Joseph, and about two miles from Platte river. It is designed to afford supplies to emigrants, and protect them from attacks of the different Indian tribes. This fort is situated in the Pawnee country. During the summer of 1849, they were in the habit of visiting emigrants, while passing through their country. As these were suffering from cholera, the disease was communicated to them, destroying great numbers. This so frightened them, that they kept at a respecful distance during the next season.

Fort Kearney is built, principally, of "adobes," (unburnt brick), usually called "doby" houses, *for short*. The great scarcity of timber, renders an expedient of this kind necessary. About two o'clock, P.M., we left the fort, and travelling about eight miles, encamped near a pool of stagnant water, about two and a half miles from the river.

We used the dried stalks of the Lobelia Inflata, as fuel at this place. There is scarcely any timber, growing on or near the banks of the Platte, except a few cotton and willow trees, and very often none even of these. The breadth of the river valley, varies from three to six or eight miles. From this point to the ford of the South Fork of Platte, a distance of 160 miles, we travelled up the river valley, suffering considerably from cold and wet weather, having no fuel but dry prairie grass, and the "Bois de Vache," or Buffalo chips, (the excrement of the Buffalo, dried by years of exposure to the sun.) These *chips* make a very good fire, when you have nothing *better*. While travelling over this part of the route, we passed hundreds of herds of this animal. The flesh of the calves and cows is very good, but that of the *elderly males* is rather *tough*. — There are also plenty of Antelopes, Bears, Wolves, Hares, Prairie Dogs, (a small animal resembling the Squirrel,) Wild Geese & Ducks, Snipes and Prairie Chickens. Several species of good Fishes are frequently found in the streams.

The rattle-snake, prairie dog and burrowing owl, are frequently found living together, amicably, in the same burrow. Natural history does not, probably, afford an example of animals so dissimilar in form and habits, occupying the same *berth*.

We reached the ford of the South Platte on the 26th of April, the weather during the whole day very cold and snowing violently. The river at this point is about one half mile in width, but very shallow, the greatest depth not being more than two feet. Later in the season, during the June rains, it is much deeper. The bed of this stream is very sandy, so much so, that if a wagon "sticks" for a few minutes, it becomes a difficult matter to get it out from the accumulations of sand.

On arriving at the opposite shore, a very inhospitable scene presented itself—large flakes of snow flying across the barren plain and bluffs, and not a vestige of any thing resembling fuel, except the Buffalo chips, which were so wetted by the melting snow as not to be in very good *burning* order. A gallon or two of "cognac," when applied *internally*, had the effect of lulling the sensibilities of a number of the company, and bringing on a state of *happy forgetfulness*. But those who drank none felt much better next morning.

This example would go far, towards establishing the position, that water is calculated to answer in all kinds of weather.

We had been compelled to leave a number of mules and horses before this time, on account of scarcity of grass and grain, and several more were added to the number, by the fatigue and exposure endured in crossing this stream.

Next day we travelled to Ash Hollow, on the North Fork of the Platte, distant 14 miles. There are several long, steep hills to descend in this distance. Before reaching the Hollow we met a train of wagons, belonging to the American Fur Company, loaded with furs and skins. On arriving at this camping place, we found plenty of wood and water; the weather was also warm and pleasant.

Between the States and this point, the road is generally very good, equal to any road of the same length in the "States."

Not supposing we would be troubled by the Indians, a number of guns were broken and thrown away at this place, our object being to lighten the loads as much as possible. After leaving the Hollow we struck the bank of North Platte, a stream entirely different from the South Fork, and the main Platte, after the junction of the two forks. The latter are wide and shallow, while the former is narrow and of considerable depth. About ten miles' travel brought us to an encampment of Sioux Indians. In these ten miles we had considerable heavy sand road.

These Indians received us very kindly, and exhibited their certificates of "moral character," and friendship towards emigrants. We, in turn, gave them some small presents. This tribe have at present about fifteen hundred lodges, each one large enough to contain five persons with their baggage. These lodges are got up in the following manner. About eight poles, about fifteen or twenty feet long, are arranged in the form of a cone; one extremity of the poles being placed around the circumference of the circle, while the other extremity forms the apex of the cone. A number of Buffalo robes dressed on both sides are sewed together, and fitted accurately to this frame work. An opening is left at the top to give exit to the smoke. This is furnished with a valve, which may be made to cover the *chimney* during rain or snow. Internally the following arrangement is observed: the fire is placed in the centre, and the baggage around the circumference of the circle, while the family occupy the intermediate space.

These Indians, as well as the tribes generally east of the Rocky mountains, are considerably skilled in the *fine* arts, making very beautiful moccasins and other articles of wearing apparel. The Buffalo robe is tanned very nicely, being white, and almost as soft as buff cassimere. — Their arms are spears and bows and arrows. A few have rifles. The Sioux and Pawnees are almost constantly at war with each other. We noticed at this encampment, a *French gentleman*, who informed us that he had been with the tribe thirty-two years.

Novelists frequently tell us of beautiful Indian maidens, but among the different tribes on the northern route to California, a pretty squaw is a *rara aris* — so rare, indeed, that I have never seen a single specimen.

They are "heavy set," and not tall enough, with broad faces and prominent cheek bones. They also, as a general thing, use too much paint, which differs too much from *carmine* to aid any in improving their complexion. They are, generally, very faithful wives, whether their husbands be Indians or whites. Nearly all the hunters and trappers in the Indian country, have one or two wives, selected from the nearest tribe. The squaws do all the "hard work," while their "lords" are busied in taking care of themselves, doing a little hunting, fishing, or fighting, when it suits their convenience.

CHAPTER THREE

Indian mode of travelling—Court House or Church—Chimney Rock—Scott's Bluff—Blacksmith Shop and Horse Creek.

fter leaving these Indians, we traveled about nine miles and encamped. Heavy sand road. During the next day we met considerable numbers of Sioux travelling toward some other encampment. Each family has one or more of a very different kind of pony, which from ill useage do not make a very *fleshy* appearance.

When about to travel, the husband takes his arms, mounts his pony, and *goes ahead*, leaving his squaw to pack up the baggage and bring up the rear. This is effected in the following manner. The lodge poles, are lashed to the saddle of a pony by one end, while the other drags on the ground. Pieces are placed across these ends of the poles, and upon them the baggage is placed. Very often two or three papooses are *piled up* on the top of the load.

If it be the only pony, it is, when all things are ready, mounted by the squaw and the *cavalcade* sets forward. — If there be a spare pony, she rides it and leads the one carrying the baggage. A variety of large dogs kept by these tribes, are also compelled to assist in these migrations. Smaller poles are attached to them, and on these, is placed, what is considered by the squaws, a just proportion of the baggage. this is a duty, which the dogs dislike very much, but the final arguments of their mistresses—kicks and cuffs—induce them to submit, after they get fairly started, these *arguments* with an occasional tzoo, tzoo, wahkashne ceit cha (get on, get on, you devilish beasts) keep them *moving*. If they be not watched, two or three of them manage to get up a fight, is soon converted into a general row, during which they get their loads off, which is quite an annoyance to the squaws, who must stop and repack them, of course *stopping the fight first*. These dogs are also highly valued as an article of food. *Dog* is considered far ahead of all *meats*, both by Indians and trappers. — Panthers is thought to be next best, while the meats we esteem most highly, are pretty far down in the list.

About forty-five miles' further travelling, over heavy sand road brought us to the "Church" or "Court House" Rock. This natural curiosity is several miles to the left of the road. It is composed of a whitish, soft rock, and, as its name imports, resembles very much, a large church or court house. Chimney Rock, seen distinctly from the "church," though twelve miles off, is also a very striking example of Nature's freaks. The lower part of this rock is shaped like a cone. The top is surmounted by a "chimney" seventy-five feet high, of almost equal diameter, through its entire length.

Height of the whole rock, two hundred and fifty feet. — This, with all the other peculiar rocks and bluffs of this part of the country, is composed of rock, similar to that of the "court house or church."

It is nearly as soft as magnesian lime stone; though not so white. Five miles farther there are a number of irregular elevations, called Scott's Bluffs. They are about five hundred feet high. When the atmosphere is clear the Rocky mountains may be seen from the summit of these bluffs. When I made the ascent the air was too hazy to get a view of these distant mountains. The main chain is about three hundred miles from the "Bluffs."

The road leaves the immediate valley of Platte river, and passes between two of these bluffs. From this to the "Blacksmith Shop," a distance of twenty miles, there is no water or wood, and very little grass. Heavy sand road part of this distance.

At the "Shop" we found plenty of red cedar timber and good water. Our corn was now nearly exhausted, and being not yet replaced by grass, we were compelled to leave stock, almost daily.

Thursday, May 22nd. left the "shop," and after travelling 12 miles crossed Horse creek, about thirty feet wide and two feet deep. In the afternoon travelled thirteen miles, and encamped on the same stream. Weather cold and windy. Next day about 10 o'clock A.M. arrived at Roubidous'. There is a blacksmith shop and stock market here. Exorbitant prices were demanded for mules or horses. As an illustration, Mr. D. Hoover, of Dalton, gave a pretty good horse and seventy-five dollars, for a rather indifferent mule. After leaving this place we traveled a few hours and encamped within four miles of Ft. Laramie. We had here plenty of good wood and water, and a little grass.

CHAPTER FOUR

Next morning (Saturday May 4th) we arrived at the fort. Finding we were going to be short of provisions, before getting through, we concluded to supply ourselves here, with a sufficient amount, but being informed by the commanding officer, that this would not be necessary, as we could get supplies at Ft. Hall, we concluded to defer the matter until arriving there. The reader will be fully apprized of the result of this determination, before we get through. Some messes got flour and hard bread, but not enough to "last through."

Mr. Joseph Sturgis of Dalton, had been suffering for days, from an attack of acute rheumatism, and as his case was not likely to be much improved, by cold weather, and the jostling of the wagon passing over the cobble-stones in the road, I advised him to remain here, until he should get well. This advice he accepted, and arrangements were made before we left for his reception at the Fort.

In a few weeks he returned to the States. Several soldiers were suffering from scurvy, brought on by the want of fresh vegetables. They were waiting for the wild onion to grow, the use of which, would soon effect a cure.

After leaving this fort we travelled twelve miles and encamped at the Warm Springs. The temperature of these springs is 66° Fahr. There are two roads leading from the springs, the left hand going by "Hebrew Springs," the right nearer the river (North Platte.) We took the latter in order to avoid crossing the "Black Hills," which in many places are very steep and the road full of cobble-stones. Next day we travelled about twenty-five miles, over a very hilly, and tortuous road, and encamped on a creek about twenty feet wide, and two feet deep. Good wood and water, and some grass here. Next day, (Monday, May 6th) we reached the La Bonte river, distance thirty-five miles. In the first fifteen miles we struck Platte River twice, in the remaining we had neither wood nor water. It snowed the greater part of this day, and the wind from the snow-capped mountains in the vicinity, was *rather fresh* to be comfortable.

The La Bonte is thirty feet wide and one and a half feet deep, with a rapid current. This stream is so called, from a hunter and trapper of the same name, whose companions were killed, and his wife Yute-chil-co-the (the reed that bends), carried away captive by the Arapahoes. This happened at the forks of the stream, while La Bonte was absent, on a trapping tour. His companions were also trapping, and coming to the forks were to await his arrival. He never recovered the "bending reed." The next morning was very cold, the thermometer at 5 o'c.

A.M. standing at 28 deg. Fahr. Five miles from the La Bonte we crossed a branch of the stream. In the vicinity of this branch there are large masses of magnesian limestone, and a peculiar earth of a deep red color. In the same locality, there is a natural, or artificial pyramid built up of "boulders" about seventy-five feet in height. — This pile of rocks looks very much as if man had been the author; but if not Dame Nature must have had "a time of it" in getting them together. Travelling sixteen miles farther we encamped on the Ala Prele river. This stream is about as large as the La Bonte. This is a very good camping place. We left encampment next morning about 2 o'clock, in order to reach the "Lower ford and ferry of north Platte," distant eighteen miles, before another company immediately behind us. We learned afterwards that this *early start* was unnecessary, as they crossed another ford, twenty-seven miles "higher up." Eight miles from ecampment we crossed the Fourche Bois river. Nine miles farther crossed Deer Creek and encamped, as the ferry boat about being built, by a gentleman from Ft. Larimie, was not quite completed. Some of the company, assisted in finishing it, in order that we might get over next day.

Deer creek is about thirty feet wide and two feet deep, with a rapid current. There are some very good fish in this stream; but "one in hand is worth two in the water" as we found that they were not easily caught. Samuel Hanson, Joseph Jackson and some others, converted a wagon cover into a fish net; but it was "no go;" the result of the fishing being a *cold bath.*

There is a coral mine a short distance from the mouth of the creek.

Next morning Wm. Palmer of Mansfield, O. had an attack of cholera morbus, but was able to resume his share of camp work in the afternoon. About noon we broke up our camp, and moved to the ferry about one mile distant, and succeeded in getting every thing over safely before night.

The North Platte at this place is about one hundred and twenty yards wide, and at this time four and a half feet deep. We encamped after crossing, having plenty of wood and some grass. There are some very beautiful volcanic rocks in this vicinity.

This ferry is one hundred and thirteen miles west of Ft. Larimie.

Friday morning, May 10th left this encampment and after travelling twenty-two miles, generally near the river, encamped five miles below "Upper Platte Ferry and Ford." During the afternoon a brown bear was killed by some of the company, not far from the bank of the river. Next morning after travelling five miles we struck the Platte for the last time.

The mineral lake and springs are seven miles farther, the waters of which are so highly impregnated with alkaline matter, as to be entirely unfit for use. After travelling about eighteen miles farther, we found a small stream of good water. There are a number of springs and creeks in this distance, but all highly alkaline.

The mules and horses that were running loose, required considerable watching in order to prevent them injuring themselves by drinking this water. This part of the country is of volcanic origin.

CHAPTER FIVE

Same subject continued.—Fording rivers—Ice springs—Rain and hail storm.

ext morning May 12th, the thermometer at 4:30 A.M. stood at 26° Fahr. After travelling two and three-fourths miles, we came to Willow Springs.—This is a good camping place, there being plenty of willows and good water. Prospect hill is one mile farther.—The Sweet Water mountains, are distinctly seen from the summit of this hill. Game is very abundant in this part of the country.

The Alkaline Lakes are about fourteen miles from "Prospect Hill." The surface of the earth here, is covered with almost pure carbonate of soda, varying from two to ten inches in thickness. This salt either for baking or any other use, is almost equal to the commercial article.—Our fuel here, and for hundreds of miles farther, was the wild sage (artimissia.) This is an aromatic shrub differing considerable from the common garden sage. The stalks are found from one fourth of an inch, to three or four inches in diameter. It does not generally grow more than three or four feet high. After growing a few years, the stalks apparently break off at the surface of the earth, and seem entirely dead, while the tops are in full vigor.—In this condition it makes very good fuel.

A bird about as large as a chicken is found among the "Sage," and is called the Sage hen.

Independence Rock is five miles from the Alkaline Lakes. This rock stands "solitary and alone" in the valley of Sweet Water River, entirely separated from the neighboring mountains. It is about five hundred feet long, two hundred broad, and about two hundred and fifty in height. It is composed of granite. We left our names in *tar* upon this rock, as thousands had done before us.—We encamped on Sweet Water about a half mile above the rock.

After leaving this encampment we forded the river—its breadth at this place about sixty feet, and depth three; and five miles farther passed the "Devil's Gate." This is a fissure in the rocks through which the Sweet Water forces its way. At the lower entrance the "gate" is nearly eighty rods in width, but becomes gradually narrower until the river forces its way through a fissure but a few feet in width. At this point the walls are four hundred feet in perpendicular height. The scenery is fearfully grand—the water roaring at your feet—the naked walls of rock apparently almost meeting, above you, while large pieces seem ready, from the slightest cause, to be detached from the parent mass, and crush you in their descent. After leaving the "gate" the road runs near the river for ten miles, six miles farther there is a very muddy creek to cross. Four miles farther the road again strikes the river. There are two roads from this point, one leading to the left over bluffs, while the other runs nearer the stream. They unite again in a few miles. The latter road is preferable as it is not so sandy. In the afternoon we travelled seven miles and encamped at the junction of the roads. — Wood and water convenient. Next morning we travelled ten miles and a half and forded the river. In the afternoon we forded twice in the distance of one and a half miles. Encamped eight miles farther, near the river bank. There is another ford here. The "ice springs" are six miles farther. Ice may be obtained here almost any time during the summer, by digging down two or three feet. — There is a very marshy piece of road in this vicinity. — We *assisted the horses and mules* through this place, and pulled the wago. through *ourselves*, mud about two feet deep. This place may be avoided by going to the left, around the source of the springs. A large train would save several hours hard work by doing this. Ten miles farther we forded the river again. In the afternoon we travelled eight miles generally near the river, fording it twice. We encamped here near a marshy spring to the right of the road.

The evening before, the mail carrier from Ft. Hall met us, and gave us the *pleasing* intelligence, that we could get no provisions at the fort, as the soldiers had been on half rations during the winter, and had gone to Oregon city, until supplies should be received from the States. — He was travelling with some Mormons from Salt Lake City. By them we sent some letters, which were to be mailed in Missouri.

Thursday May 16th, travelled in the forenoon fifteen miles to a branch of Sweet Water, crossing in the distance several small streams. We also passed a poplar grove a short distance to the left of the road. We had some trouble fording the branch, as there was a bank of snow, ten or fifteen feet deep, on each side. We forded a short distance below where the snow was not so deep. We *exercised* ourselves for a while, carrying rocks through the stream, *barefoot*, and placing them near the opposite bank, in order to get the wagons through more easily. Temperature of the water 32°. In the afternoon we were detained several times by snow banks. We travelled only seven miles, and encamped for the last time on Sweet Water. While getting supper we were visited by a rain and hail storm which abruptly concluded the *cooking* operations.

CHAPTER SIX

*"South Pass,"—Separation,—Green River,—Ham's Ford.—A Supper.—
Snow Road—Soda or Beer Springs—Steamboat Springs.*

Next morning we forded the river, which was considered swollen by rain, and melting of the snow. The wagon belonging to the Canton mess, was overturned in the stream and their provisions considerably damaged.

Nine miles travel over a very good road brought us to the South Pass or summit of the Rocky mountains. This is about nineteen miles in width, with a very gradual ascent. Many pass over the mountains here, without sixty feet high, and sixty rods apart, will point this out, as they are very near the dividing ridge.—This "Pass" is about nine hundred miles west of St. Joseph. Altitude 7490 feet lat. 42°27′ N. Long. 109°27′ W.

The Pacific Springs are three miles west of the "Pass," Pacific Creek one mile farther. This is one of the head branches of the Colorado river, which empties into the Gulf of California. The Dry Sandy is nine miles farther.—Junction of the Oregon and Salt Lake roads, six miles farther.

At this point our company was divided, a few going by Salt Lake in order to get some provisions. But the majority thought they could get through with the amount on hand. If we had taken the Ft. Bridger road to Ft. Hall we might have travelled together for some distance farther, but this is a roundabout way, about seventy-five miles farther, than by "Sublette's cut off."

The Little Sandy is five miles from the junction. Here we encamped, that is the greater part of the company.—As our captain had just left (going by Salt Lake, all discipline was suspended.) and a part of the company, principally from Holmes county, O., travelled a few miles farther before encamping. A day or two after, we elected J. Weirick, of Dalton, captain, and something like order was again restored. Next morning (Sunday May 19th,) we left Little Sandy, and forded the Big Sandy five miles farther.

As there is no water and very little grass, between this and Green River, distant 35 miles, we rested until one o'clock, P.M., in order to prepare our stock for this long drive. We likewise supplied ourselves with a considerable quantity of water.

We encamped, after travelling about 14 miles. This part of the road is tolerably level, but somewhat sandy in places. No fuel but wild sage. Next morning at 3:30 A.M. we left the encampment and reached Green river about noon. There are several very long, steep hills to ascend and descend in this distance.

As the river had not yet risen much, we were able to ford it. There are two islands in it at this ford. Width about 300 yards. This is a very dangerous stream to cross, owing to its width, depth and rapidity of current. It is rarely fordable during the months of June and July. Numbers are drowned annually in attempting to cross it. We rested here until next morning. In the evening we had a *cotillion party.* Our *spacious room* was illuminated, by lighting two or three dozens of sperm candles, and arranging them in the form of a circle.

Soon the violins were tuned up, and the *performances* commenced. The evening's entertainment was concluded. by singing a few songs. Unfortunately none of the "gentler sex" was present.

Some of those who were in the best spirits on that evening, have long since found graves west of the Sierra Nevada.

Next morning we left the ford, and travelling about six miles, struck a branch of Green river coming in from the north-west. The road in this distance is very tortuous, in one place going about a mile and a half in order to make about sixty rods: but the *peculiarities* of the country rendered this necessary. After striking this branch, we followed it about six miles, and crossed it. Rather difficult on account of the swollen state of the stream.

In the afternoon we travelled about thirteen miles, in a direction south of west, and encamped near the foot of some high bluffs, partially covered with snow.

At this place the Lamison and Peffer messes threw away their wagons and "went to packing." This is a very fine camping place—plenty of fir timber and snow water.

Next day eighteen miles travel brought us to Ham's fork of Green river.

This we found impossible to ford, on account of its swollen state. A wagon bed was, therefore, launched, and S. Coe and J. Mendenhall, Esq. *put aboard* to paddle it across. The rapidity of the current carried it under, and those on board swam ashore. A number followed it down stream, and recovered it about a half a mile below.

We then lashed two together, with a similar result. Nothing more towards ferrying was done this day. In the evening a supper was "got up," by the Hanson & messrs. Smith messes, of which quite a number partook.

Wild goose, wild duck, speckled trout, *dumplings, flapjacks,* hard bread, stewed fruit and coffee, comprised the "bill of fare." Next day was spent in getting logs from the mountains, and constructing a ferry.

Next morning the ferry was launched, the ropes arranged, and in a few hours **every thing was safely landed on the opposite bank. The horses and mules swam** across, without any loss. This stream is about fifty feet wide and six deep. Later in the season it is much shallower. Next day we travelled about twenty miles, over a very rough road, and encamped in Bear river valley, about three miles from the stream. During this day we were compelled to cut a road through the snow 83 yards long and four feet deep.

Next day (Sunday, May 26th,) we had several snow storms. About noon we forded Thomas' fork of Bear river. The Fort Bridger road unites with that through Sublette's cut off at this place. In the afternoon we travelled about 16 miles, and encamped near another branch of the river, about ten feet deep, but the current not rapid. Next day we ferried with an ordinary wagon bed.

The wagons being unloaded were drawn thro' the stream by ropes. Rather a laughable adventure occurred, while doing this. A wagon was started into the stream with two or three in it. It soon began to sink, and went down until the tops of the bows were the only parts above the surface. Terror was depicted on the visages of those in the wagon, who not being acquainted with the exact depth of the stream, seemed afraid that they too might get *lower than the surface*. We encamped about one mile from this crossing. We now had good grass generally, and the stock was beginning to improve. Wild flax is found in this valley. Wild sage for fuel. Next morning we crossed some bluffs, and struck the river in six miles. Encamped twenty-one miles further down, — road very good. Several small streams to cross. Next day about noon we came to the "Soda Springs," 15 miles farther. They are about half a mile north of the road. The water is impregnated with carbonic acid, which gives it the property of holding certain minerals in solution. As it issues from the surface it loses this gas, and the minerals are precipitated. By this process large mounds of calcareous matter have been formed.

This water, on analysis, yields the following products:

Carbonate of Lime,	92.50
do. Magnesia,	.50
Silica, Alumina, and loss,	7.90
	100.00

With the addition of any of the vegetable acids, this makes very good Soda water.

Steam Boat Springs is about one mile lower down, and very near the bank of the river. The water is thrown from an orifice in the rock, to the height of several feet, with a kind pulsatory or puffing motion.

In chemical constitution this water is somewhat similar to that of the Soda springs.

About four miles further the road leaves Bear river valley, and turns to the right, crossing, twenty miles further, a dividing ridge, which separates the waters of the Pacific from those of the Great Basin. We encamped near a spring of sweetish water, issuing from a bed of volcanic matter. This is about eight miles from the Soda or Beer springs.

Next night we encamped near the summit of the ridge last mentioned. We had several showers of rain during the night. Grass, good water and "sage," plenty.

Next day, when about three miles from encampment, we met a number of Indians and half breeds, who had some very good mules and horses to sell or *trade*. Our company made a number of exchanges, and bought several horses. About twenty miles further we encamped near Fort Hall, crossing several small streams. The last eight miles, heavy sand road and marshy streams.

CHAPTER SEVEN

here are two forts at this point; the upper one belonging to the United States, the lower to the Hudson Bay Company. They are about five miles apart. No supplies are to be obtained at either place, except *bacon* and *whiskey*, — the later at six dollars per gallon. I think the establishment belonging to the United States, was deserted a few months since, probably on account of the severity of a number of the winters. We were informed that several hundred horses had died, during the winter of '49 and '50, from cold and want of food. Mr. Grant of the lower fort, received us very kindly, and gave milk to those of the company who applied for it, for which he would receive nothing. This was the first we had seen since leaving the States.

These forts are situated on Lewis' Fork of the Columbia river, about 1,300 miles from St. Joseph.

At this time and for about ten days previously, great numbers of the Company were suffering from "Rocky Mountain Fever," peculiar to these mountains. It is very mild, and brief in its duration, rarely requiring more than a dose of calomel followed, if necessary, by a few doses of Dover's Powder or Ipecac. Aside from this we were all in the enjoyment of excellent health.

We left these forts about 9 o'clcok, A.M. (June 1st.) and about noon forded the Port Neuf river seven miles below. This stream is about one hundred yards wide, and four feet deep. The opposite bank is rather marshy. — The Panack River is seven miles lower down — would not be difficult to ford, but for its miry banks. There is a spring of good water six miles farther, in the valley of Lewis river. Here we encamped. We had cosiderable marshy road during this day.

Next morning, five miles travel brought us to the American Falls on Lewis River. The water falls thirty or forty feet over an irregular mass of rocks. A visit to the falls will amply repay the traveller for his trouble. Fall River is seventeen miles farther. This derives its name from the number of falls near its mouth. Many of them are old beaver dams petrified. It is about thirty feet wide and two feet deep. The descent to, and ascent from, the stream are pretty steep. We encamped on Raft River about eight miles farther. Good road this day.

Some who have written "Guides to California" describe the road from Ft. Hall to this river as being a very bad one, but if they were to travel it, they would hardly find the *desperate* places they describe. There is only one or two ravines in this distance and they are not at all troublesome.

Next morning forded the river at encampment and reforded one mile farther. Between these two fords we left the Oregon Road, which kept to the right, following for a considerable distance, Lewis or Snake river.

Fourteen miles from the second ford we again crossed it. The stream here is about twenty-five feet wide, and five feet deep. Being too deep to ford we made a bridge by drawing two wagons into it, and on these we carried across the baggage. The road on both sides of the stream at this crossing, is very marshy. Mud in many places from twelve to eighteen inches deep. Goose Creek is nine miles farther. We encamped here — plenty of wood, water and grass. Hedgepeth's cut-off comes in at this point. This "cut-off" leaves the road about four miles west of Soda Springs, and goes by a more direct route to Goose Creek. Probably twenty-five or thirty miles are gained by taking this "cut-off," but after all very little time is gained by it.

The weather at this time was pretty cool, especially in the morning, the thermometer at 5 o'clock A.M. generally from two to six degrees below the freezing point of water.

Next day towards evening we passed the "Castle Rocks," quite an assemblage of fantastically shaped rocks. Some *enterprising* traveller has painted the word "hotel" or "City Hotel" *in tar* on one of them. The "hotel" is sufficiently large *externally*; but the accommodations at present are rather *slim*.

The road from Salt Lake city, comes in about three miles from the "rocks."

We encamped near a small stream one mile farther. — Plenty of red cedar wood, also good grass. Provisions were now becoming rather *scarce*, and we began using as a *substitute*, a weed or "greens" that is very abundant. — Though not as *nutritious* as a great many other things, we could at least "fill up" on it.

Permit us now to stop a short time, while we pen a few words in reference to the "Salt Lake Valley," after which we will resume the thread of our narrative. At the junction of the Oregon and Salt Lake roads, eighteen miles west of the South pass, the latter strikes off in a south west direction, crossing Big Sandy, Green River, Ham's Fork, and Black's Fork, from thence over the dividing ridges, separating the waters of the Gulf of California from those of the Great Basin. There are a great many streams to cross, and the country generally is very mountainous. — The city is situated between the Salt and Utah Lakes, and very well watered, artificially, by a small stream from the neighboring mountains. Though hemmed in by mountains the valley is very fertile, yielding good crops, of wheat and other grain. Mechanic Shops and mills have been built, and are in operation, and every thing seems to be in a very flourishing condition. It is settled principally by the Latter Day Saints or Mormons. There are large quantities of rock salt and other minerals in the neighboring mountains. Near the city there are hot, cold, and tepid springs within a few feet of each other, which afford great facilities for bathing establishments.

The Great Salt Lake north of the city of considerable extent, but from late reports is very shallow, its greatest depth being but a few feet. It has no outlet but by evaporation. Its waters are strongly impregnated with saline matter; five gallons in the month of September or October yields fourteen pints of salt, being almost if not altogether, a saturated solution. The country west of the lake is barren and sandy, *producing* nothing in many places, but saleratus. There is a trail leading west from the city, intersecting the road from Ft. Hall on Humboldt river, but the country is so inhospitable, that few travel it. The ordinary road leads north from the city, intersecting the other, ninety miles below Ft. Hall. We will now resume our narrative.

CHAPTER EIGHT

Rattle Snake River—Hot Springs—Humboldt River—Sink—Lawson Route—Rabbit Wells—Desert—Hot Springs—Mud Lake.

Next day sixteen miles travel brought us to Rattle Snake river; and, after travelling fifteen miles, we encamped near the stream.

In the next forty-five miles, we found the road generally pretty good and water and grass plenty. At this point we passed a number of hot springs. Temperature near that of boiling water. The soil in this part of the route is strongly charged with alkaline salts. We were detained near the springs two or three hours, by a marshy piece of road. The ford of Humboldt River is forty miles farther. We crossed several marshy streams a few miles east of this ford. We arrived here June 8th, about noon. The river here is about thrity feet wide and six feet deep. We ferried it in a wagon bed. After loading up, and traveling half a mile, we were again detained by a very swampy branch of the river. We took the mules and horses from the wagons through ourselves. This consumed the balance of the afternoon, and we therefore encamped. —About dark we were visited by a storm of rain for which we were well prepared, having already thrown away tents, wagon covers, and extra clothing. We had supposed these things, would be no longer required, as a "guide" we had with us, contained the expression, "it seldom rains here."

Next morning we crossed another branch about a mile from camp. This was not so miry as the other. There is another branch about twenty miles farther, about one hundred feet wide and three feet deep. Not difficult to ford. Encamped near the river seven miles farther. We had some grass here, but did not, as yet, see the line of cotton wood and willow trees, which is said to mark the course of the river. About 21 miles farther the road forks, the left hand one keeping near the stream, crossing it a number of times, while the other does not cross it at all. Early in the season the river road can scarcely be travelled on account of the swollen state of the stream. The two roads frequently intersect each other. We encamped fifteen miles farther after crossing another small branch. Distance to day about thirty-six miles. Next forenoon we travelled about twelve miles and stopped near a spring of good water. Good grass here. This is on the bluffs several miles from the river. We generally had much better grass on these than in the immediate valley of the river.

From some cause we did not find much of the "blue grass, herds grass, clover and other nutritious grasses," with which the valley is said to be "beautifully

80

clothed."

We encamped on the river fifteen miles farther. Grass poor. Cold rains nearly all day. "The great heat of the sun, and continued clouds of dust did not trouble us *very much*".* Next day we travelled about twenty-seven miles, generally near the river. Grass poor. Surface of the earth with alkaline salts. Small branches in this vicinity, are about the color of *good lye* from ashes. The whole country in wet weather, smells like an old *ashery.* — Grease Wood, a small, scruggy, prickly, ugly bush, comprises the *timber* in many places. Where this grows you will rarely find anything else.

Travelled next day thirty miles, generally some distance from the river — country a sterile waste, not "furnishing the requisite for the emigrants' comfort in abundance"†.

Cold and rainy all day.

Travelled next day about sixteen miles, finding pretty good in several places, sage for fuel. Rain and snow during the night.

There is another very miry branch about 20 miles further. We crossed about a mile above the ordinary ford. Depth of stream three feet. Mud on the opposite bank about two feet. Here we again drew the wagons through by manual force.

Encamped in the river valley three miles farther. Next day we travelled about 24 miles, generally near the river. We could not travel in the immediate valley on account of the swollen state of the stream. The low bluffs are fatiguing, on account of the depth of the sand. We arrived at the point last mentiond, about 5 o'clock, P.M., and concluded we could go a short distance further.

Eight miles further, over a barren plain, we encamped, without any wood, water or grass. As we had nothing to cook by, and very little to cook, supper was dispensed with. Evening cold and rainy.

Leaving camp before breakfast, we reached the river again about sunrise — distant six miles from encampment.

We might remark here, that Humboldt river empties, or loses itself, in a marshy lake, surrounded with bullrushes, called the "Sink"; and from the features of the country we considered it not far distant.

We rested here until one o'clock P.M., supplying ourselves with water and grass, to use while crossing the Great Desert.

Five miles farther we left the river, expecting to strike Truckies, or Salmon Trout, in forty miles. Instead of taking this road we should have gone on to the Sink, seventy-five miles farther, then across the desert to Truckies, or Carson river, and from thence across the mountains, to Johnson's or Bear river, or Hangtown, near the American.

---

†Ware's guide to California, page 33.

But fortunately, or unfortunately, we took the Lawson, or *Green Horn's* cut off, which is farther than the other routes — but the road is better. There are also more and better grass and water.

We left the river about four o'clock P.M., and travelled about 15 miles. After getting seven or eight miles from the river, we found good grass at a number of points.

Next day, about noon, we arrived at the "rabbit wells," sixteen miles further.

We found pretty good water in the wells, — but later in the season it is unfit for use.

There are hundreds of ox skeletons between the river and these wells, which had died the previous season, from lack of food, there being very little good grass after the first of July. Bunch grass is the principal article of food in this part of the route. This, in the proper season, is very nutritious, being almost equal to oats or corn. It ripens about the middle of June. An hour's drive from the wells, brings you to the desert proper — a vast plain entirely destitute of vegetation.

The sand is very light and porous — the mules and horses sinking in six or eight inches, when it is perfectly dry. This, with the continued clouds of dust, renders travelling fatiguing and unpleasant. The road is strewed with wagons and every other species of property. The carcasses of oxen are scattered every where. Owing to the heat and dryness of the atmosphere, these do not undergo putrafaction, but become dry and hard, leaving the animal almost entire.

The stillness of death reigns over this vast plain, — not the rustling of a leaf or the hum of an insect, to break in on the eternal solitude. Man alone dares to break it. The desert, on the different routes, varies in width from twenty to fifty miles.

The "Hot Springs" are about twenty-one miles from the "rabbit wells." There is some grass near them. The main one is about twelve feet in diameter, and probably one hundred feet deep. Water perfectly transparent, — temperature that of boiling water. Meat may be boiled in a few minutes.

There are other springs and wells in the vicinity, but the water, late in the season, is too brackish to be fit for use. The road between the springs and Mud lake is pretty sandy, — very little grass or water, — distance 25 miles. We encamped here Wednesday evening June 19th.

About three miles from encampment we gained the summit of a bluff. There is said to be pure silver scattered over this. There is a small lake about two miles farther, to the left of the road. A short distance from the lake the road enters a very narrow, rocky ravine, or valley — very narrow and tortuous in many places — with perpendicular rocks on each side, several hundred feet in height.

There is a small stream of good water and good grass in this valley. It is about twenty miles in length. A few miles from the ravine we found a few gallons of good vinegar, which had been left by some emigrant. This was quite an addition to the "greens."

We encamped about thirty miles from the exit from the last mentioned valley. In this distance we passed a number of small lakes, which line the western rim of the "Great Basin." Next morning we stopped and breakfasted on *greens, oats, &c.,* near some hot springs about two miles from encampment. We stopped at the base of the Sierra Nevada, six miles farther, crossing a marshy valley containing several lakes.

CHAPTER NINE

We travelled along the base of the mountains about six miles before beginning the ascent.

During this time, and for days before, several members of the company thought we were on the road to Oregon, or *some* place *else* than California and advised the expediency of going back. This probable would not have been proposed, had it not been, that we were almost entirely out of provisions. But the majority were for going ahead, let the road lead where it would, as some mules might be killed for food, did things become desperate.

About three miles from the beginning of the ascent, the Salem and Hanson messes with the exception of J. Mendenhall and J. Campbell, took the "back track" for Humboldt River, distance one hundred and fifty miles, having to recross the desert, and again cross it on the "Carson" or "Truckie" route.

We began ascending the mountain about four o'clock, P.M. and encamped for the first time west of the "Sierra Nevada," or snowy mountain. It is very steep at this pass, but not so rocky as at the Carson or Truckie.

It was not found necessary to double any of the teams.

The scene from the summit is grand in the extreme.—Lofty ranges of mountains, are seen distinctly though distant hundreds of miles. Their summits crowned with eternal snow, and their sides with dense forests of pine and cedar. Owing to the dryness and purity of the atmosphere, the outline of the most distant object is distinctly marked. All the varied scenery of the four seasons are recognized at a single view. The valleys clothed with vegetation, the mountain tops presenting all the indices of perpetual winter. Between these two extremes is every variety of climate.

Next morning (Sunday 23d.,) discovering indications of marshy road ahead, we concluded to make "this the last day with the wagons," and begin packing. Accordingly the wagons were converted into pack-saddles as soon as possible, extra baggage thrown away, and by noon we were again "en route."

During the afternoon we travelled along the eastern shore of Pitt Lake, and encamped opposite the southern extremity of it.

Distance this afternoon eighteen miles. Next day about noon we reached Pitt river. Eighteen miles further. Ten miles further we forded it, and encamped four miles further.

We were detained in the afternoon by a case of poisoning. Mr. Daniel Rudy, of Stark county, O., eat rather plentifully of a root, which in taste and appearance resembles the fat of hogs. This proved a very violent emetic, and might produce death in certain cases. Some were quite elated, when the root was discovered; remarking that they could "now have fat to cook with the greens," — but the result of the first experiment crushed their *brilliant* expectations.

Next day we travelled about thirty miles, fording the river several times.

Road considerably marshy. We avoided this by travelling on the neighboring bluffs. During the day we noticed several Indian signal fires, but did not anticipate an attack from them. A few hours undeceived us. Next morning, some time before day light, a party of Digger Indians, killed, wounded and drove off, more than half of the stock belonging to the company, without making any attack upon ourselves.

We had not been apprehending any trouble from these tribes, and had no one on watch. This carelessness, together with our being nearly without arms, rendered it a very easy matter to accomplish the robbery. A few remained at camp in order to pack the baggage, or part of it, on what horses and mules remained, while the balance went in search of any that might be found in the vicinity. We were to meet about three miles further. About one mile from camp we found the body of "Spot," a splendid mare belonging to the messrs. Hoovers of Dalton. She had borne, well, the fatigues of the journey, and had rendered us signal service the evening before, while crossing the stream. The Indians had carried away part of the carcass, and some of our company took a part of that which was left. About ten o'clock A.M., we met at the place before designated, and held a "council war."

It was determined that our *only gun* should, if possible, be brought into *shooting order* — a service which it had *ceased* to perform for some time previously. A similar decree was passed upon what pistols we had.

It was also determined that R.F. Cahill and Wm. McConnell should take horses, and go ahead to the nearest settlements, and return with some provisions, while we in the meantime should hurry along as fast as possible. They accordingly set out with about one pound of provisions, consisting of boiled corn, scraps of hard bread, and dried apples, *mixed together*. We travelled about six miles further, and stopped for *dinner*. Bill of fare boiled corn and *horse beef!* (We had reserved some corn and oats to feed the stock while crossing the desert; but as it was not required, we began boiling it for our *own* use.)

While *dining* Cahill and M'Connel returned, informing us, that they had overtaken an Oregon train which was a few miles ahead, and from which we might get some provisions. We learned that we were yet about two hundred miles from the settlements. We at once started forward regardless of road or rocks, and overtook the Oregonians about 5 o'clock, P.M. At our request they prepared some supper, for which we paid them one dollar per pound for flour and bacon and fifty cents for shorts, and could not get a sufficient supply at these rates.

We thought these rates very high, and as some of them required some medical attention, our fees were made to correspond to a certain extent with *theirs*, an arrangement which seemed to *grind* some of them considerably. At this place we crossed Pitt River for the last time. On this river there is a rock of pure carbonate of magnesia, about one hundred feet in height—enough to supply the world for ages. It is as pure and light as the commercial article. There are also near the source of the river—some very peculiar crystalized rocks, some of them, two four-sided pyramids applied base to base.

About two days, after we were robbed by the Indians; the Canton mess consisting of seven or eight persons were killed at the same place. They had been travelling with us until about the time we struck Humboldt River, but their team giving out they were compelled to drive more slowly. They encamped on the river (Pitt.) and during the evening were attacked. One was killed. Next morning they were visited by a few, who by signs informed them, that in order to secure themselves form another attack, they should at once leave their encampment and move forward. This they declined doing, as they were determined to bury their friend, and wait for the Messrs. Childs and Miller, who were a short distance behind. In a short time they were attacked by a larger number, who took from them every thing they had, leaving them entirely naked. They were then ordered to swim the stream, but before reaching the opposite shore were, with a single exception, killed by a shower of arrows. At this moment the report of a gun in the vicinity, caused them to retreat precipitately, leaving George Stuck, of Canton, in the stream, among the bushes lining its banks, badly wounded.

Miller and the Childs' coming up in a few moments, rescued him from his perilous situation, gave him clothing, and brought him to Lawson's. The gun of which we had spoken had been fired at a dove, by one of the Childs.—Stuck remained near Lawson's for a short time, but being supplied with funds he started for home. While in San Francisco he was attacked by diarrhea or dysentery and died. These Indian tribes have been warring with the whites, especially the Oregonians, for a number of years, each party destroying one or more of the other, when ever an opportunity presents itself. This accounts for these attacks These tribes are great cowards and never make an attack, unless the odds are greatly in their favor. We had thrown away our arms and were therefore unprepared to resist the most feeble attack. These Indians were severely chastised by several companies from California settlements, during the last summer.

CHAPTER TEN

Getting Short again—A party of "Prospectors"—Feather
River meadows—Deer Creek—Lawson's.

fter purchasing our provisions, and making inquiries in reference to the road we again set forward, and after travelling sixteen miles encamped on Pitt River in company with the Oregonians. Some were already complaining of being sick; but when it is remembered that we had been living on almost nothing for some time, it is readily supposed that entirely too much was eaten when the opportunity presented itself, and derangement of the digestive organs, might as a matter of course, be expected to result.

Friday, June 28th. Left encampment, and at once entered on a piece of marshy ground of ten miles in breadth. Depth of mud from one to three feet. Encamped twelve miles farther,—wood, water and grass, plenty.

Next two days travelled about forty miles and encamped near a small lake; in company with a party of "prospectors" a term applied to those, in search of "diggins."

Our supply of provisions growing "short" we were again on *rations*. We were presented with some fresh venison, by the miners. They informed us that the mining districts generally were crowded, that provisions had become much cheaper, and people in general not growing rich very fast.

Next day we travelled about twenty-eight miles and encamped near "Feather River Meadows." Next morning left encampment very early and arrived at the ford about sun rise, distant three miles. The river runs through the valley here, in two different branches. Early in summer, the entire valley one and a half miles in width, is entirely covered with water. The branches were about four feet deep, the remainder of the valley varied from one to three feet of mud and water. Cold, wet, and hungry, we stopped on the opposite bluff, to prepare and eat our scanty breakfast. The following scene will give the reader an idea of our *financiering* in cookery.

A. Clark, M. Hoover, and *ourself* were cooking for ourselves and eleven others belonging to the mess. Our stock of provisions, consisted of a lot of musty tea, a few pounds of flour and a few dried elder berries. Hoover made the tea, while Clark and I made the *soup* and *dumplings*,—the preparations of the latter articles, being by *experimental philosophy*, deemed the most economical method of disposing of the flour. A handful of the berries were put into two camp kettles holding about six gallons of water.—These gave *color* and *consistency* to the *soup*. A small quantity of flour was then made into a stiff batter. This was carefully divided by a spoon into a certain number of pieces, corresponding to the number of individuals in the mess.

The result of this *ceremony* was always announced in order that each one might learn, the amount of his share. I suppose any one might have eaten the entire amount, of course excluding a portion of the six gallons of tasteless soup.

Next day, forenoon, travelled two miles, and *dined* on musty tea alone.

Encamped fourteen miles farther, in "Little Valley," on Deer Creek.

Next day about noon we stopped at a small stream, the last water we had until reaching the valley of the Sacramento River. In the afternoon and night, we, or least some of us, reached dry creek in the valley, distant thirty miles—the road mountainous and rocky. A few got through to water, but the majority were scattered along the road for several miles, worn out by hunger, thirst, and fatigue.

Next day Thursday July 4th, about noon, we encamped on Deer Creek about half a mile from Lawson's Rancho.

We got up a Fourth of July dinner on musty hard bread, and beef bones in a state of *incipient putrefaction,* which was highly relished by us, as any of the more *sumptuous* repasts, served up to our friends in the States.

We were received, and treated very kindly by a party of miners, who were *jerking* beef in the vicinity of our camp.

From this time the members of our company began to separate, and in a few days were as a general thing, hundreds of miles apart. Those who came by the Salt Lake, Carson and Truckie routes, reached Sacramento Valley about the time we did.

CHAPTER ELEVEN

Native Gold—Where found—methods of obtaining it.

This metal is obtained pure, or in combination with silver, copper, iron, palladium, or tellurium. It is also found combined with the sulphuret or oxide of iron. When melted and thrown up by Volcanic agency, it is found in every possible variety of shape. When crystalizing it generally assumes the form of the cube or octohedron.

Its feeble affinity for oxygen prevents it from tarnishing, and by property is readily detected, when in combination with those metals that do not so highly, possess this property. Geologically it is found in granite, quartz, mica, slate, syenites, green stone, and trachyte. In the mines of California generally with quartz.

Small grains or larger pieces are observed studding the surface of the latter rock, but many specimens contain considerable quantities, which cannot be detected by the senses.

In order to obtain it the rock is pulverized, triturated with quicksilver, which readily unites with it, and the compound being washed out, the quicksilver is distilled off, leaving the gold in the retort.

Gold is not acted upon by nitric, sulphuric, or chlorhydic acids, while many of the other metals are. When combined with silver, copper or iron, the compound may be placed in one of the acids, which acts upon these, while the gold remains unaffected. The *aqua regia* of the old chemists, a combination of nitric and chlorhydric acids, will dissolve it, though not affected by either one separately employed.

Gold is found in California, in fine dust, or in pieces weighing from a grain to several pounds. That from the middle Fork of the American River, and Feather River, in the latter part of its course, is generally in the form of scales, and is very pure.

From the North Fork of Feather River and some other streams, in irregularly shaped lumps, frequently, coated with black oxide of iron.

The gold from the "Kayote" diggins on Deer creek contains, I believe some silver, and is not worth more than fourteen dollars per ounce, while that from other "diggins" is worth from sixteen to sixteen and a half.

This metal is generally sought for and obtained in the mountainous parts of the country, in the bars along the streams, or the gulches or ravines along the mountain sides—The former constitutes the "wet" the latter the "dry" diggins.

The "wet" are worked during the latter months of summer after the water has fallen enough to expose the bars. The "dry" during the rainy season when the ravines have water in them. Small quantities of fine gold may be carried down the rivers near their mouths, but in quantities too inconsiderable to make it an object to wash it out. During the summer of 1850 the majority of miners were engaged in "daming" the streams, supposing that valuable deposits would be found in their beds, but these generally failed, scarcely one in ten paying expenses. — Many who were in possession of several thousand dollars in the spring, found themselves when the dams were completed, without any thing, and deeply in debt.

In order to obtain the "dust," the soil, sand, and shingle is dug out from among the rocks, placed in a pan or washer, and washed off, the gold from its great specific weight being precipitated to the bottom. If the gold be fine, mercury is mixed with the dust, their affinity causing them to unite at once. The amalgam is then placed in a retort and the mercury distilled off.

Machines are being erected in many places to crush quartz rock, many specimens of which yield from twenty-five to fifty cents per pound. This in the course of a few years will be the principal business carried on by gold hunters, as the bar and ravine washings, are as a general thing, pretty well worked out.

The gold mines of the far west, occupy quite an extensive region — Gold is obtained from many of the rivers of Oregon — from the Salt Lake country, — the eastern slope of the Sierra Nevada, and from nearly all the streams in Upper California.

The vast amount of this metal in the possession of the Montezumas, at the time Mexico was conquered by the Spaniards, had been obtained, most probably, in the mountains on the Gila River. The Indian tribes in this part of the country, seem to have some knowledge on this point, and make every effort to prevent the whites from exploring the country.

They are also in possession of certain traditions, which say these mines were once extensively worked, and yielded large quantities of Gold.

The roughness of the country and hostility of the Indians have as yet prevented many from exploring it.

It should not be undertaken by less than a company of thirty men, armed with revolvers, with good mules and plenty of provisions. Even then, it would be trip attended with extreme danger and privation.

CHAPTER TWELVE

Climate of California,—its Cause,—Soil,—Productions,—Animals, &c.

The climate of California is considerably milder that at the same latitude on the Atlantic coast. The whole Pacific coast of North America follows the same law; the difference in temperature being equal to ten or fifteen degrees of latitude. The following theory will, probably, explain satisfactorily the cause of this difference. Large tracts of highland, in or near the polar regions, serve as vast magazines of cold, which exert a chilly influence on countries at considerable distances from them. The large tracts of land north and north-east of British America, no doubt, exert this effect upon the Atlantic coast, and U. States proper; while the country on or near the Pacific coast, is not subject to such an influence. Water especially, when in a large body, exerts an equalizing effect on the climate of a country—moderating the cold of winter and heat of summer; preventing what are called "excessive climates."—The North Pacific, probably, exerts an effect of this kind.

There are, properly, but two seasons in California—the "wet" and "dry."

It generally begins to rain between the first of November and latter part of December, and continues until about the middle of April. There are frequent intermissions, during which the weather is as mild as during our April.—Grass, and vegetation generally, begins to grow at the commencement of this season.

From the middle of April until the ensuing "winter," there is generally no rain—the sun being unobscured by clouds for months at a time. Owing to this, vegetation begins to suffer about the middle of June.

During the months of July and August the temperature is frequently as high as 140° in the sun, and 110 or 112° in the shade. But owing to the dryness of the atmosphere, this exalted temperature is not more sufferable than that of 75° in the "States"—this condition of the air promoting a rapid evaporation.

An individual perspiring freely, feels comfortable during the hottest months.

There is scarcely ever any dew, especially in the valleys.

The climate of this country is certainly as pleasant as any in the world.

Occassionally there is but very little rain during the wet season,—and if this be the case, vegetation the ensuing season is apt to suffer very much. The last winter has been one of this description. Fifteen years ago there was a similar one. Great number of cattle perished during the next summer for want of grass.

seven feet in height, and half an inch in diameter.

Last year's oat stalks made good *walking sticks!* Good crops of potatoes, turnips, radishes, melons, squashes, cucumbers and tomatoes, are raised without much labor.

The mountains are thickly covered with pine and cedar, (*pinas colorado, and pinas monophyllus)* but the country is too rough and cold for agricultural purposes.

The principal animals are black tailed deer, antelope, elk, coati, generally called "Kayotes." and last though not least the Grizzly Bear. The principal domestic animals, are Spanish cattle and horses, with a few hogs and sheep.

There are plenty of deer, antelope and elk, in all parts of the country — the indolence of the natives preventing them from hunting them, and the rich pastures affording food to multitudes of them.

The coati, an animal belonging to the wolf family, is found in great numbers.

The grizzly bear is found in or near the mountainous districts. This animal, in color, somewhat resembles the buffalo, the extremeties are short, but supplied with muscles of immense power. The feet are supplied with massive claws, designed for tearing up roots rather than for scratching. The average weight may be put down as eight hundred pounds, though some have been killed weighing over two thousand!

They are very tenacious of life, and cannot be entirely disabled at once, unless the ball penetrates the brain. A dozen balls may be driven through the most important organs of the body, and they are still able to fight three or four men.

They are not disposed to begin an attack; but when aroused, or wounded, are rather *ugly game.* The hunter, when on foot, should not attack them, unles there be a tree near, on which he may take refuge. The flesh of this bear is superior to beef or buffalo.

The horses, generally, are descendants of those brought to Mexico by the Spaniards. They are of the ordinary size, active, and capable of enduring a great deal of fatigue. Immense numbers were at the different "ranchos," or farms, prior to the discovery of the gold mines, and were then worth almost nothing.

Some proprietors owned from fifteen to twenty-five thousand. If a horse was hired, they were generally satisfied, if the saddle and bridle were returned.

The Spanish cattle make much better beef than ours, — though living on nothing but grass. They are, generally, pretty wild, and require the *lasso* to capture them.

Some are very docile, and may be taught to be of essential service in driving cattle.

Neal has an ox which will lead a beef to any butcher's establishment, however distant; keeping it in the road, and standing apparently unconcerned, while it is knocked down and bled. He is then sent home alone. When his services are again required, he must be *lassoed* — to avoid which he makes every effort to secrete himself among the bushes.

There are plenty of wild fowl, such as wild geese and ducks, quails, sandhill cranes, &c.

The rivers abound in fish, of the salmon family, varying from two to four feet in length. The markets of this country are well supplied with nearly every variety of *flesh, fish, or fowl.*

The time for making rapid fortunes, by gold mining, has gone by; but those who desire a pleasant home in the far west, will be as well satisfied with this country, as any other west of the Rocky mountains.

CHAPTER THIRTEEN

*The "Diggers"—Habits—Religion, &c.,
Mexicans—a Fandango—Chief Towns*

The Indians of California belong to what is called the Digger tribe. They live upon roots, grass, *bugs, grasshoppers,* acorns and fish. Acorns are gathered in great quantities, pounded into a kind of meal, and baked. This, with dried fish, constitutes their principal food.

They go entirely naked—their *birth-day* suits lasting all their lifetime. Their houses are little better than large ovens, built in the following manner: A hole is dug from twenty to fifty feet in diameter, and about four feet deep—a frame work placed over this, and the whole covered with dirt. An opening is left at one side, to crawl in and out at. They are almost entirely destitute of horses, dogs, or any other domestic animal. The bow and spear are their only weapons.

A predatory warfare is carried on between the different tribes, generally between the "mountain" and "valley" tribes.

As they are not blessed with much property, real or personal, squaws are about the only spoils of victory.

Numbers of these are carried away, as captives, when a "ranchere" or Indian village is taken.

Their religion is pagan, worshipping trees, water, earth, &c. Their *fandangoes* are religious ceremonies. Several are held during each year, and are considered very important occasions. During the day numbers of them, collect at some particular *ranchere* to make preparations for the "scene" at night.

Their naked bodies are painted in every variety of style, and their hair tied up, and covered with feathers, pieces of cloth, beads &c. About dark a small fire is built in the center of a large hut, giving just enough light to make *darkness visible.* Around this fire, fifty or sixty collect, and the dance or tramp begins, keeping time with their hands, arms, head and nearly every part of the body.

The music is a short chant, kept up by the dancers, though the greatest noise is produced by the tramp of their bare feet on the soft earth.

They have a musical instrument, which is simply a tube, having a couple of holes in it, flute like, to produce the *modulations*. It resembles neither a bugle, flute, clarinet, flagelet, or any thing else, *except another* one of *the same kind.*

I think the playing of this instrument is almost beyond the "ken" of any thing connected with civilization.

When the temperature of the "oven" is about 150°, and the perspiration running in streams off the bodies of the actors, the whole thing resembles more the midnight orgies of demons, than any thing *human*.

When an individual dies, a hole is dug at the mouth of his hut, the body put in and covered, after which, his property is laid on the grave and burned.

The mourners keep up a dismal howling for several days. This is the general custom, though some tribes burn the body and scatter the ashes to the winds.

They are passionately fond of gambling, and never quit the game, until one of the parties is *dead broke*. The game is played in the following manner.

Two having seated themselves on the ground opposite each other, the one takes a small pebble, and passing it from one hand to the other requires the other, to tell in which hand it is.

If he fails to tell, one is counted on the game, if otherwise the other takes the pebble. Seven constitutes the game. They are fond of intoxicating drinks, are great cowards, and generally dishonest.

Many have been kept at the Catholic missions and have in this way acquired some knowledge of the Spanish language.

The Mexicans are indolent and superstitious. They have two or three phrases which are almost constantly in use.

If asked to do any thing, they *no quiere* (don't care or don't want to.)

To almost every question, even the most simple, you get the answer *quien sabe* (who knows) or I don't know.

The following anecdote will illustrate their ignorance or carelessness. A gentleman seeing a girl carrying a child, and wishing to enter into conversation asked her the question: *Queiere es le padre de esta, senorita* (who is the father of this, senorita, pointing to the child) *quien sabe senor* (who knows, sir.)

They are too indolent to raise much grain or vegetables, being content to live on beef, onion, garlic and pepper.

They are very pious during their attendance at church, but bring their chickens with them; tying them outside until the services are concluded in order to save the *labor* of returning home for them.

After services are over cock and bull fighting consume the balance of the day. A Fandango *comes off* in the evening. This about sums up a Mexican's idea of life. For cowardice they cannot be beaten any where.

A Comanche Indian would almost think he was *compromising his dignity*, by fighting one of them.

We will conclude by giving the situation and commercial importance of some of the principal cities and towns. San Francisco situated on a bay of the same name a few miles from its mouth, is the largest town in the state, contains many good buildings of brick and iron. It has the best harbor in the world, and is the

95

principal port on that part of the coast.

Sacramento City on the Sacramento River, 175 above San Francisco is the second place in the state. The river is navigable for the largest vessels the greater part of the year. In commercial importance it almost equals San Francisco. Freemont is a small place situated on Sacramento River just below the mouth of Feather River. — Marysville at the junction of Feather and Yuba Rivers, is growing rapidly, and is in a very flourishing condition. — Small streams ply between it and Sacramento city during the greater part of the year. It is fifty miles by land above the latter place.

Nevada city is situated on Deer creek forty miles above Marysville.

Hangtown is near the American River, about fifty miles above Sacramento city. Three men were hung here in one day for stealing, and from this the place derives its name. Stockton and Benicia are situated on the bay of San Francisco.

They are places of considerable importance. There are a few towns in the southern mines but we are unacquainted with their situation, and importance.

GUIDE TO CALIFORNIA
BY THE
OVERLAND ROUTE.

TO THE EMIGRANT.

ou are about to undertake a long, tedious, and somewhat dangerous journey; and it is highly necessary that you should be acquainted with the *minutiae* of the route, and the outfit required, in order to take you safely and expediously to the land of your destination. Without these it would be an adventure attended with insuperable difficulties.

Endeavor to make an early start—do not wait for grass; but carry along grain sufficient to supply your stock until "grass comes." Start from the Missouri river as early as the first of April, and you will get through soon enough, be detained less by streams, and have better grass in the latter part of the route.

In reference to the starting point, St. Joseph is probably as good as any you may select. You can procure nearly every article necessary for the outfit; the road is good, and the distance to the Platte river less, than from Weston, Kansas or Independence.

A mess of 6 persons should provide themselves with 3 wagons, and 12 mules or horses. Mules not less than 6 or 8 years old are preferable. Two of said wagons should be light 1 horse ones. In these load your provisions, clothing, (just enough to take you through) and other necessary baggage. The other may be a common two horse wagon—on which load forty of fifty bushels of corn, oats or barley. If you can, put a few extra bushels on your light wagons. See that these are well made; have the wheels high, and the beds water tight.

Thus equipped you need not wait for grass. Be careful that you do not start with any unnecessary baggage; if you do you will throw it overboard before you get half way through. The road at present is strewed with nearly every thing from a steam engine to a child's cradle, that has thus been disposed of.

The following amount of provisions will be sufficient for a mess of six persons:

Flour	500 lbs.	Pepper	1 lb.
Hard Bread	250 do.	Sugar	100 do.
Bacon	500 do.	Molasses	10 gals.
Corn Meal	60 do.	Dried Fruit	2 b.
Coffee	30 do.	Carbonate Soda, (for baking)	2 lbs.
Tea	5 do.	Chocolate	10 do.
Rice	10 do.	Pickles	1 small keg

need not be afraid of Indians, until you get on the latter part of the route.

The Pawnees, Sioux, Crows and Snakes, will most probably treat you civilly enough, if you observe the Golden Rule. The "Diggers" on Humboldt river and **Upper California**, may attempt to injure you, or your stock, but the *report* of a gun will generally sufficiently *frighten them.*

You should provide yourselves with gum elastic sacks, to carry water on those parts of the route where it is scarce. Every mess should have a saw, auger, and a few nails.

Be careful that you do not form too large a company, — thirty men are enough.

Do not be in too much haste in electing officers. Travel a few days — become thoroughly acquainted with each other; then elect a captain in whom you are prepared to place the utmost confidence. As soon as each mess gets ready to start, cross the river, and encamp near the bluffs, six miles from St. Joseph.

While here examine every thing connected with your outfit. See that every thing is in order, and that no indispensable article has been forgotten.

In camping arrange the wagons in the form of a circle. During the evening the stock may be staked outside, and not bro't within the enclosure until the night watch is placed.

You want a complete camp kettle, coffee pot, frying pan, tin plates and cups, knives, forks and spoons. The frying pan will do to bake *flap jacks*, a very good kind of bread; not very *digestible*, but probably as much so as any other you will *get up*.

One gun, with a pound or two of powder, will be sufficient for each mess. You

From the bluff take the right hand road		"Warm Springs"	5
From this point to Big Blue, (road good, and a sufficient number of camping places)	120 miles	Good Camping place	17
		(Take the right hand road from the springs.)	
To Platte Valley	190	Creek (good camp)	8
Fort Kearney	10 — 320	(Easily forded.)	
(Road good, wood scarce. Part of this distance you travel near the Little Blue.)		Platte River	8
		Do.	7
South Platte ford	175	La Bonte River (20 ft. wide — 2 ft. deep)	20
(Road level — buffalo chips for fuel.)		(Road hilly and scarcely any water.)	
Ash Hollow (good encampment.)	14 miles.	Branch of La Bonte	5
Court House Rock	68	A La Prela River (good camp)	15
(Heavy sand road in many places.)		Fourche Bois (40 ft. wide — 2½ ft. deep)	8
Chimney Rock	12	Platte River	4
Scott's Bluffs	5	Deer Creek (good camp)	5
"Black Smith Shop"	22	North Platte Ferry	1 — 776
(Water scarce in this distance.)		Camping place	12
Horse Creek	12	(Some heavy road)	
Camping place	12	Upper Ferry of North Platte	15
Ft. Larimie and Larimie River	4 — 666	Small Stream	25
Long Hill to descend	7	(In this distance you pass a number of lakes	
(4 miles from the fort take the left hand road.)		and springs; but the water is so charged with	

alkaline matter as to be unfit for use.)	
Willow Springs	2¾
Prospect Hill	1
Small Creek	8¼
Alkaline Lakes	6¼
Sweet Water River	4¼
Independence Rock	3¾
Sweet Water Ford	1
Devil's Gate	4
Creek	½
Do.	½ mile
Miry Do.	6
Sweet Water River	4
(Take right hand road.)	
Sweet Water	3
Sage Creek	2
Good Camp	3
Creek	2
Road leaves the River	2
Strikes it again (ford—2½ ft. deep.)	6
Ford and reford	1½
Ford (some heavy road)	8
Ice springs	5¾
Alkaline Swamps	¼
Ford	10
Branch of Sweet water	½
Summit of hill	1¾
Ford	2
Reford	½
Creek and spring (good camp)	3
Hilly road for	3
Creek	3
2 Small creeks in next	2 miles
Strawberry creek	2
Quaking Aspen creek	1
Branch of Sweet Water	2¾
(May 16th 1850 10 feet snow)	
Willow Creek	2¼
Sweet Water ford	4¾
South Pass	10—949
Pacific Springs	3
Do. Creek	1
Dry Sandy (no water in this distance.)	10
Junction of Oregon and Salt Lake roads	
(Right hand road to Ft. Hall.)	6
Little Sandy	5
Big Sandy	5
(May 19, 1850 — 40 ft. wide—2½ ft. deep.)	

Green River	35
(No water in this distance.)	
Ford the river at the islands. Strike the upper point of second one, then the shore. Bold stream, generally dangerous to cross.	
Muddy creek	2½
Branch of Green River	4½
(Road hilly and crooked.)	
Ford of this branch	5
(May 21st, 1850—60 feet wide—3½ deep— current rapid.)	
"Bluffs" (good camp)	12
Ham's Fork of Green River	17
(Road hilly—water plenty.)	
(May 22nd, 60 feet wide—8 ft. deep— current rapid.)	
Grove of Timber	12
Small stream	4
Bear River valley	4
(Small stream here to the right of the road.)	
Thomas' Fork of Bear (ford.)	12
(If you cannot cross at the ordinary ford, go half a mile higher up.)	
Branch (road good water plenty.)	17
(May 27th, 40 feet wide—7 ft. deep)	
Foot of Bluffs	1
Bear River	5
Creek 2 ft. deep (road good)	6
Camp (water plenty, road good)	15
Beer or Soda Springs	15
Steamboat Springs	½
Road leaves the River	4—1151
(Take the right hand road to Ft. Hall. The left is "Hedgpeth's Cut-off" strikes the other road about 70 miles below Ft. Hall.)	
Small Stream and Volcanic Spring	4 miles
(Good camping place.)	
Creek (Road good.)	8
Miry Stream	7
Summit of Ridge	5
Ft. Hall (marshy or sandy road.)	25—1200
Trading Station of Hudson's Bay Co.	5
Creek 60 ft. wide	3
Ford of Port Neuf (100 yds. wide—4 ft. deep.)	4
Panack River (somewhat miry)	7
Spring to the right of the road	6
American Fall on Lewis River	4
Good camping place (2 or 3 ravines.)	10

Small Rocky Stream	1	Again touches the river	14
Fall River ford (30 ft. wide—2 ft. deep.)	6½	(No wood water or grass.)	
Raft River ford (good camp.)	7½	Junction of the Lawson and Truckie routes	5
Reford	1	Camping place (by the latter route.)	35
(Oregon road between these fords.)		Slough of Humboldt River	15
Third Ford of Raft River	14	"Sink" of do.	20
(marshy near the river)		(The best water is in a slough that passes	
Goose creek	9	through a bend and narrow bluff.)	
Ford of Do.	5	From the Sink to Hot Springs	20
Good camp	9	(No grass or water.)	
Do. (mountainous.)	14 miles	Truckie River (no grass or water.)	25 miles
(Pass the "Steeple Rocks" in this distance. The		Ford (good camp.)	5
trail from Salt Lake City intersects the road		Bend in the river (good camp.)	15
about 1 mile before reaching the last mentioned		Travel up the river	8
camp.)		Cross a hill to the river	12
Creek (several small streams in this distance)	16	Pass creek Kanyon	42
Follow this creek (Road good.)	21	(Good camps every few miles.)	
Small stream	12	**Through the Kanyon**	5
Follow it	8	Red Lake (good camp near.)	11
Cross the bluffs and reach a creek	12	Lake Valley (good camp.)	6
Hot Springs	7	Over the ridge to Rock Valley (good camp.)	10
Marshy Road for	1½	Sick Springs	13
Camp	5	Camp Creek (poor camp.)	10
Summit of a ridge	2	**Pleasant Valley. Gold mines**	28
Tolerably good camping place (soil alkaline)	18	Sutters	55—1957
Two miry streams	5	(Lawson Route. The road on this route is	
Humboldt or Mary's River ford	9—1424	better, grass and water better, and not much	
Miry branch	½	farther than the other.)	
Branch	½	From Humboldt to "Rabbit Wells"	30
Branch 100 ft. wide—3 ft. deep	20	(No water, but good grass in many places.)	
(Some good grass in this distance.)		Hot Springs (no water nor grass.)	20
Right hand road leaves the River	28	Mud Lake (very little water nor grass.)	20
Small creek	10	Summit of a bluff	2
Crossing of Small stream	3	Small Lake	3
Spring of good water	12	Through a Kanyon	20
Road strikes the river (grass poor.)	15	(Good grass and water.)	
Branch	12	Summit of Sierra Nevada	45
Road strikes the river (grass poor.)	12	(Several marshy valleys containing lakes in this	
Alkaline Stream (grass poor.)	3	distance.)	
Road strikes the river	10	Camp	1½
Leaves it	2	Valley of Pitt Lake	4
Again touches the river	6	Camp	10
Miry branch (good road.)	18	Pitt River	18
(You will find a better ford one mile above the		Ford of Pitt	10
ordinary one.)		Second ford	7
Road strikes the river	2	Third	25
Road leaves the river	25	Last Ford (several fords in this distance)	15
(Some good grass in this distance.)		Camp on the river	16

100

Do. Do. (road marshy)	10	Camp	10 miles
Camp	10	Lawson's Rancho	35
Do.	10	(very little water and bad road.)	
Spring	8	Potter's Rancho	25
Small Lake and meadow	22	Neal's	8
(Not much water in this distance.)		Hamilton City	18
Feather River ford and meadows	31	Yeats' Rancho	8
(Plenty of water.)		Yuba City and Marysville	12
Good Camp	10	Sacramento City	50
"Little Valley" and Deer creek	14	San Francisco	175
By the Lawson Route to Sacramento city		−2146	

DISTANCE FROM ST. LOUIS TO CALIFORNIA VIA. NEW MEXICO

To Independence	400	San Louis Rey	46
Crossing of Big Arkansas	350	Pueblo de los Angelos	100
Bent's Fort	225	Santa Barbara	100
Sante Fe	270	Montery	310
Rio Del Norte at San Phillpi	30	Rio Selina	15
Descending Right Bank (Rio Del Norte)	210	Rio San Joaquin	85
Copper mines	75	Rio Tuwaleme	12
River Gila	40	Rio Stanishlow	10
Pimo Village	500	Sutter's Fort	90 − 3314
Mouth of Gila	165	From San Francisco to Panama	3600
Crossing Colorado	10	Across the Isthmus	87
Do. Cornado	100	To New Orleans	1600 − 5287
First Ranchero in California	65	From New York to San Francisco via	
San Diego	45	Cape Horn	17000

101

INDEX

103

104

105

COLOPHON

The JOURNALS OF SAMUEL RUTHERFORD DUNDASS AND GEORGE KELLER, *was printed in the workshop of Glen Adams, which is located in the sleepy country village of Fairfield, southern Spokane County, Washington State. The text was set in type by Kristy Mayfield and Dale La Tendresse using a 7300 Editwriter computer photosetter. The setting is in eleven point Baskerville roman with running heads in ten point Baskerville Bold caps and page numbers in twelve point Baskerville Bold. Camera-darkroom work was by Evelyn Foote Clausen. The film was stripped, opaqued and plates made by Robert La Tendresse, who also printed the sheets using a 770CD Hamada offset press. The sheets were folded by Sydney Stevens Jr. using an air-operated Baum folding machine. Indexing was by Edward J. Kowrach. General book design was by Glen Adams who also did the color imprinting using a 14x22 open platen press, a Chandler & Price, vintage 1928. Assembly of the books was by the Ye Galleon Press staff. The paper stock is sixty pound Simpson Opaque in a wove finish. Binding is by Willem Bosch of Oakesdale, Washington. This was a fun project. We had no special difficulty with the work.*